HOUGHTON MIFFLIN HARCOURT

Expressions
Common Core

Dr. Karen C. Fuson

GRADE

5

Volume 1

This material is based upon work supported by the
National Science Foundation
under Grant Numbers
ESI-9816320, REC-9806020, and RED-935373.

Any opinions, findings, and conclusions, or recommendations expressed in this material
are those of the author and do not necessarily reflect the views of the National Science Foundation.

 HOUGHTON MIFFLIN HARCOURT

VOLUME 1 CONTENTS

UNIT 1 Addition and Subtraction with Fractions

UNIT 2 Addition and Subtraction with Decimals

UNIT 3 Multiplication and Division with Fractions

UNIT 4 Multiplication with Whole Numbers and Decimals

Student Resources

Dear Family,

Your child is learning about fraction concepts. Using fraction bars, students learn about unit fractions, or fractions that are just one part of the whole, such as $\frac{1}{2}$ or $\frac{1}{4}$.

$$\frac{1}{4} \;+\; \frac{1}{4} \;+\; \frac{1}{4} \;+\; \frac{1}{4} \;=\; \frac{4}{4}, \text{ or 1 whole}$$

Non-unit fractions are sums of unit fractions.

Unit fractions are used to convert mixed numbers, which have a whole-number part and a fraction part, to fractions in which the top number (numerator) is larger than the bottom number (denominator).

$$\frac{3}{4} = \frac{1}{4} + \frac{1}{4} + \frac{1}{4}$$

$$2\frac{1}{4} = \frac{4}{4} + \frac{4}{4} + \frac{1}{4} = \frac{9}{4}$$

Fraction bars help students understand how to compare, add, and subtract fractions with like denominators.

Share with your family the Family Letter on Activity Workbook page 1.

$$\frac{a}{d} + \frac{b}{d} = \frac{a+b}{d}$$

$$\frac{1}{4} + \frac{2}{4} = \frac{3}{4}$$

$$\frac{a}{d} - \frac{b}{d} = \frac{a-b}{d}$$

$$\frac{3}{4} - \frac{1}{4} = \frac{2}{4}$$

If $a > b$, then

$$\frac{1}{a} < \frac{1}{b} \text{ and } \frac{a}{d} > \frac{b}{d}$$

$$\frac{1}{3} < \frac{1}{2} \text{ and } \frac{3}{7} > \frac{2}{7}$$

These skills extend to fractions with unlike denominators. We rewrite each fraction with a common denominator, using multiplication to make an equivalent fraction.

$$\begin{array}{c} \times 5 \\ \frac{1}{3} = \frac{5}{15} \\ \times 5 \end{array}$$

We add and subtract mixed numbers by treating the whole-number part and the fraction part separately, ungrouping 1 whole, if needed.

$$\begin{array}{rcl}
& & 3\frac{20}{15} \\
4\frac{1}{3} & = & 4\frac{5}{15} \\
-2\frac{7}{15} & = & 2\frac{7}{15} \\
\hline
& & 1\frac{13}{15}
\end{array}$$

Sincerely,
Your child's teacher

COMMON CORE This unit includes the Common Core Standards for Mathematical Content for Number and Operations—Fractions, 5.NF.1 and 5.NF.2, and all Mathematical Practices.

Estimada familia:

Su niño está aprendiendo conceptos de fracciones. Al usar barras de fracciones, los estudiantes aprenden acerca de fracciones unitarias es decir, fracciones que son solo una parte del entero, como $\frac{1}{2}$ ó $\frac{1}{4}$.

$$\frac{1}{4} + \frac{1}{4} + \frac{1}{4} + \frac{1}{4} = \frac{4}{4} \text{ ó 1 entero}$$

Las fracciones que no son unitarias son sumas de fracciones unitarias.

$$\frac{3}{4} = \frac{1}{4} + \frac{1}{4} + \frac{1}{4}$$

Las fracciones unitarias se usan para convertir números mixtos, los cuales tienen una parte formada por un número entero y una parte formada por una fracción, a fracciones en las que el número de arriba (numerador) es mayor que el número de abajo (denominador).

$$2\frac{1}{4} = \frac{4}{4} + \frac{4}{4} + \frac{1}{4} = \frac{9}{4}$$

Las barras de fracciones ayudan a los estudiantes a comprender cómo se comparan, se suman y se restan las fracciones con denominadores iguales:

$$\frac{a}{d} + \frac{b}{d} = \frac{a+b}{d}$$

$$\frac{1}{4} + \frac{2}{4} = \frac{3}{4}$$

$$\frac{a}{d} - \frac{b}{d} = \frac{a-b}{d}$$

$$\frac{3}{4} - \frac{1}{4} = \frac{2}{4}$$

$a > b$ así que

$$\frac{1}{a} < \frac{1}{b} \text{ y } \frac{a}{d} > \frac{b}{d}$$

$$\frac{1}{3} < \frac{1}{2} \text{ y } \frac{3}{4} > \frac{2}{4}$$

Estas destrezas se aplican también a fracciones con denominadores distintos. Volvemos a escribir cada fracción con un denominador común, usando la multiplicación para obtener una fracción equivalente.

$$\frac{1}{3} \xrightarrow{\times 5} \frac{5}{15} \xleftarrow{\times 5}$$

Sumamos y restamos números mixtos tratando la parte del número entero y la parte de la fracción por separado, desagrupando 1 entero si es necesario.

$$\begin{array}{ccc} & & 3\frac{20}{15} \\ 4\frac{1}{3} & = & 4\frac{5}{15} \\ -2\frac{7}{15} & = & 2\frac{7}{15} \\ \hline & & 1\frac{13}{15} \end{array}$$

Atentamente,
El maestro de su niño

Muestra a tu familia la Carta a la familia de la página 2 del Cuaderno de actividades y trabajo.

COMMON CORE   Esta unidad incluye los Common Core Standards for Mathematical Content for Number and Operations— Fractions, 5.NF.1 and 5.NF.2, and all Mathematical Practices.

Introduce the MathBoard

Use Activity Workbook page 3.

VOCABULARY
equivalent fractions

▶ Find Equivalent Fractions by Multiplying

You can use a number line to find **equivalent fractions**.

Circle the unit fractions up to $\frac{2}{3}$. Complete the number lines and equation boxes to find equivalent fractions for $\frac{2}{3}$.

1. Sixths

$$\frac{2 \times \boxed{}}{3 \times \boxed{}} = \boxed{\frac{}{6}}$$

2. Ninths

$$\frac{2 \times \boxed{}}{3 \times \boxed{}} = \boxed{\frac{}{9}}$$

Use Activity Workbook page 4.

▶ Find Equivalent Fractions by Multiplying (continued)

Circle the unit fractions up to $\frac{2}{3}$. Complete the number lines and equation boxes to find equivalent fractions for $\frac{2}{3}$.

3. Twelfths

$$\frac{2 \times \boxed{}}{3 \times \boxed{}} = \frac{\boxed{}}{12}$$

4. Fifteenths

$$\frac{2 \times \boxed{}}{3 \times \boxed{}} = \frac{\boxed{}}{15}$$

5. Eighteenths

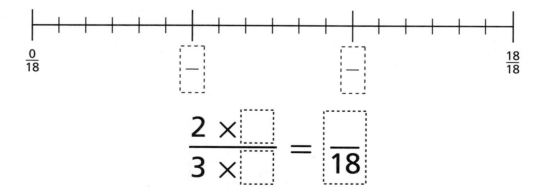

$$\frac{2 \times \boxed{}}{3 \times \boxed{}} = \frac{\boxed{}}{18}$$

6. You **unsimplify** a fraction by multiplying the numerator and denominator by the same number to make more but smaller unit fractions. The number you multiply both parts of the fraction by is called the **multiplier**. Discuss how you unsimplified $\frac{2}{3}$ in Exercises 1–5. What was the multiplier in each exercise?

Explain Equivalent Fractions

Use Activity Workbook page 5.

VOCABULARY
simplify

▶ Find Equivalent Fractions by Dividing

Complete the number lines and equation boxes to show how to simplify each fraction to $\frac{2}{3}$.

7. Fifteenths

$$\frac{0}{15} \qquad\qquad \boxed{-} \qquad\qquad \boxed{-} \qquad\qquad \frac{15}{15}$$

$$\frac{10 \div \boxed{}}{15 \div \boxed{}} = \frac{2}{3}$$

8. Twelfths

$$\frac{0}{12} \qquad\qquad \boxed{-} \qquad\qquad \boxed{-} \qquad\qquad \frac{12}{12}$$

$$\frac{8 \div \boxed{}}{12 \div \boxed{}} = \frac{2}{3}$$

9. Ninths

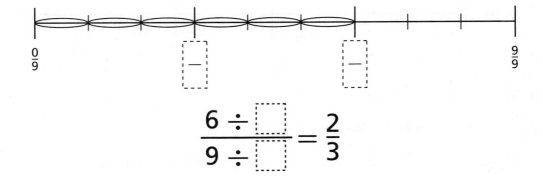

$$\frac{0}{9} \qquad\qquad \boxed{-} \qquad\qquad \boxed{-} \qquad\qquad \frac{9}{9}$$

$$\frac{6 \div \boxed{}}{9 \div \boxed{}} = \frac{2}{3}$$

10. When you simplify to make an equivalent fraction, you divide the numerator and denominator by the same number to make fewer but bigger unit fractions. Discuss how that has happened for Exercises 7 through 9 above.

11. Discuss how simplifying and unsimplifying are alike and different.

► Solve Real World Problems

Henri needs to make $\frac{2}{3}$ of his free throws in order to make the basketball team. Answer Exercises 12–14 about Henri's throws.

12. If he throws 12 times, how many baskets does he need?

13. If he throws 9 times, how many baskets does he need?

14. If he throws 15 times, how many baskets does he need?

► Practice Using Equivalent Fractions

Use the number lines to complete Exercises 15–18.

Fifths

Tenths

Fifteenths

15. What fraction is marked by the car?

16. What fraction is marked by the airplane?

17. If you worked $\frac{4}{5}$ of an hour, how many tenths of an hour did you work?

18. Which is greater, $\frac{2}{5}$ or $\frac{4}{15}$? How do you know?

Explain Equivalent Fractions

Use Activity
Workbook page 6.

▶ Use the Multiplication Table to Find Equivalent Fractions

You can use these multiplication tables to find equivalent fractions.

×	1	2	3	4	5	6	7	8	9	10
1	1	2	3	4	5	6	7	8	9	10
2	2	4	6	8	10	12	14	16	18	20
3	3	6	9	12	15	18	21	24	27	30
4	4	8	12	16	20	24	28	32	36	40
5	5	10	15	20	25	30	35	40	45	50
6	6	12	18	24	30	36	42	48	54	60
7	7	14	21	28	35	42	49	56	63	70
8	8	16	24	32	40	48	56	64	72	80
9	9	18	27	36	45	54	63	72	81	90
10	10	20	30	40	50	60	70	80	90	100

×	1	2	3	4	5	6	7	8	9	10
1	1	2	3	4	5	6	7	8	9	10
2	2	4	6	8	10	12	14	16	18	20
3	3	6	9	12	15	18	21	24	27	30
4	4	8	12	16	20	24	28	32	36	40
5	5	10	15	20	25	30	35	40	45	50
6	6	12	18	24	30	36	42	48	54	60
7	7	14	21	28	35	42	49	56	63	70
8	8	16	24	32	40	48	56	64	72	80
9	9	18	27	36	45	54	63	72	81	90
10	10	20	30	40	50	60	70	80	90	100

$$\frac{3}{5} \quad \frac{6}{10} \quad \frac{9}{15} \quad \frac{12}{20} \quad \frac{15}{25} \quad \frac{18}{30} \quad \frac{21}{35} \quad \frac{24}{40} \quad \frac{27}{45} \quad \frac{30}{50}$$

$$\frac{4}{7} \quad \frac{8}{14} \quad \frac{12}{21} \quad \frac{16}{28} \quad \frac{20}{35} \quad \frac{24}{42} \quad \frac{28}{49} \quad \frac{32}{56} \quad \frac{36}{63} \quad \frac{40}{70}$$

1. Color rows 4 and 9 in the first table. Use the table to complete the equivalent fractions for $\frac{4}{9}$.

$$\frac{4}{9} = \frac{\blacksquare}{\rule{1cm}{0.4pt}} = \frac{\blacksquare}{\rule{1cm}{0.4pt}} = \frac{\blacksquare}{\rule{1cm}{0.4pt}} = \frac{\blacksquare}{\rule{1cm}{0.4pt}} = \frac{\blacksquare}{\rule{1cm}{0.4pt}} = \frac{\blacksquare}{\rule{1cm}{0.4pt}} = \frac{\blacksquare}{\rule{1cm}{0.4pt}} = \frac{\blacksquare}{\rule{1cm}{0.4pt}} = \frac{\blacksquare}{\rule{1cm}{0.4pt}}$$

2. Color rows 3 and 8 in the second table. Use the table to complete the equivalent fractions for $\frac{3}{8}$.

$$\frac{3}{8} = \frac{\blacksquare}{\rule{1cm}{0.4pt}} = \frac{\blacksquare}{\rule{1cm}{0.4pt}} = \frac{\blacksquare}{\rule{1cm}{0.4pt}} = \frac{\blacksquare}{\rule{1cm}{0.4pt}} = \frac{\blacksquare}{\rule{1cm}{0.4pt}} = \frac{\blacksquare}{\rule{1cm}{0.4pt}} = \frac{\blacksquare}{\rule{1cm}{0.4pt}} = \frac{\blacksquare}{\rule{1cm}{0.4pt}} = \frac{\blacksquare}{\rule{1cm}{0.4pt}}$$

Complete these equivalent fractions.

3. $\frac{1}{4} = \frac{\blacksquare}{\rule{1cm}{0.4pt}} = \frac{\blacksquare}{\rule{1cm}{0.4pt}} = \frac{\blacksquare}{\rule{1cm}{0.4pt}} = \frac{\blacksquare}{\rule{1cm}{0.4pt}} = \frac{\blacksquare}{\rule{1cm}{0.4pt}} = \frac{\blacksquare}{\rule{1cm}{0.4pt}} = \frac{\blacksquare}{\rule{1cm}{0.4pt}} = \frac{\blacksquare}{\rule{1cm}{0.4pt}} = \frac{\blacksquare}{\rule{1cm}{0.4pt}}$

4. $\frac{1}{3} = \frac{\blacksquare}{\rule{1cm}{0.4pt}} = \frac{\blacksquare}{\rule{1cm}{0.4pt}} = \frac{\blacksquare}{\rule{1cm}{0.4pt}} = \frac{\blacksquare}{\rule{1cm}{0.4pt}} = \frac{\blacksquare}{\rule{1cm}{0.4pt}} = \frac{\blacksquare}{\rule{1cm}{0.4pt}} = \frac{\blacksquare}{\rule{1cm}{0.4pt}} = \frac{\blacksquare}{\rule{1cm}{0.4pt}} = \frac{\blacksquare}{\rule{1cm}{0.4pt}}$

Use Activity
Workbook page 7.

► Split Fraction Bars

Use the fraction bars to find equivalent fractions for $\frac{3}{4}$.

$\frac{3}{4}$

5.

$\frac{}{8}$

Multiplier = [ ]

$\dfrac{3 \times [\ ]}{4 \times [\ ]} = \dfrac{[\ ]}{8}$

6.

$\frac{}{12}$

Multiplier = [ ]

$\dfrac{3 \times [\ ]}{4 \times [\ ]} = \dfrac{[\ ]}{12}$

► What's the Error?

Dear Math Students,

I tried to find a fraction equivalent to $\frac{5}{6}$.
I multiplied the denominator by 2 to make
smaller unit fractions. This can't be right
because $\frac{5}{6}$ is almost 1, and $\frac{5}{12}$ is less than $\frac{1}{2}$.
Why doesn't my method work?

Your friend,
Puzzled Penguin

$$\frac{5}{6 \times 2} = \frac{5}{12}$$

7. Write a response to Puzzled Penguin.

VOCABULARY
greater than, >
less than, <
unit fraction

▶ Like Denominators or Like Numerators

The **greater than** symbol, >, and the **less than** symbol, <, show how two numbers compare.

$27 < 72$ Twenty-seven is less than seventy-two.

$10 > 3 + 4$ Ten is greater than three plus four.

In this lesson, you'll use these symbols for fraction comparisons.

Same Denominator If two fractions have the same denominator, then they are made from **unit fractions** of the same size. The fraction with more unit fractions is greater.

Example: $\frac{3}{5} < \frac{4}{5}$

Same Numerator If two fractions have the same numerator, then the number of unit fractions is the same. The fraction with the larger unit fractions is greater.

Example: $\frac{2}{5} > \frac{2}{7}$

Compare.

1. $\frac{4}{9}$ ⬤ $\frac{4}{7}$ 2. $\frac{2}{10}$ ⬤ $\frac{1}{10}$ 3. $\frac{1}{5}$ ⬤ $\frac{1}{3}$

4. $\frac{5}{8}$ ⬤ $\frac{6}{8}$ 5. $\frac{3}{7}$ ⬤ $\frac{3}{8}$ 6. $\frac{5}{7}$ ⬤ $\frac{6}{7}$

VOCABULARY
common denominator

► Unlike Denominators

If two fractions have different denominators, you can compare them by first rewriting them as equivalent fractions with a **common denominator**. You can use different strategies to do this, depending on how the denominators are related.

Case 1: One denominator is a factor of the other. **Possible Strategy:** Use the greater denominator as the common denominator.	**Example:** Compare $\frac{3}{4}$ and $\frac{5}{8}$. Use 8 as the common denominator. $\frac{3 \times 2}{4 \times 2} = \frac{6}{8}$ $\frac{6}{8} > \frac{5}{8}$, so $\frac{3}{4} > \frac{5}{8}$.
Case 2: The only number that is a factor of both denominators is 1. **Possible Strategy:** Use the product of the denominators as the common denominator.	**Example:** Compare $\frac{4}{5}$ and $\frac{5}{7}$. Use 5×7, or 35, as the common denominator. $\frac{4 \times 7}{5 \times 7} = \frac{28}{35}$ $\quad$ $\frac{5 \times 5}{7 \times 5} = \frac{25}{35}$ $\frac{28}{35} > \frac{25}{35}$, so $\frac{4}{5} > \frac{5}{7}$.
Case 3: There is a number besides 1 that is a factor of both denominators. **Possible Strategy:** Use a common denominator that is less than the product of the denominators.	**Example:** Compare $\frac{7}{9}$ and $\frac{5}{6}$. 18 is a common multiple of 9 and 6. Use 18 as the common denominator. $\frac{7 \times 2}{9 \times 2} = \frac{14}{18}$ $\quad$ $\frac{5 \times 3}{6 \times 3} = \frac{15}{18}$ $\frac{14}{18} < \frac{15}{18}$, so $\frac{7}{9} < \frac{5}{6}$.

Compare.

7. $\frac{1}{5}$ ⬤ $\frac{2}{7}$

8. $\frac{15}{18}$ ⬤ $\frac{5}{6}$

9. $\frac{3}{8}$ ⬤ $\frac{5}{12}$

10. $\frac{1}{5}$ ⬤ $\frac{3}{20}$

11. $\frac{5}{8}$ ⬤ $\frac{3}{5}$

12. $\frac{3}{10}$ ⬤ $\frac{2}{8}$

Strategies for Comparing Fractions

▶ Special Cases

You can *always* compare two fractions by rewriting them so they have the same denominator. However, in some special cases, you can compare the fractions more efficiently just by using reasoning.

Special Case 1: Both fractions are close to $\frac{1}{2}$. **Possible Strategy:** Compare both fractions to $\frac{1}{2}$. If one is less than $\frac{1}{2}$ and one is greater than $\frac{1}{2}$, the fraction greater than $\frac{1}{2}$ is greater.	**Example:** Compare $\frac{5}{8}$ and $\frac{2}{5}$. Compare both fractions to $\frac{1}{2}$. $\frac{5}{8} > \frac{1}{2}$ $\qquad$ $\frac{2}{5} < \frac{1}{2}$ So, $\frac{5}{8} > \frac{2}{5}$.
Special Case 2: Both fractions are close to 1. **Possible Strategy:** Compare both fractions to 1. The fraction closer to 1 is greater.	**Example:** Compare $\frac{5}{6}$ and $\frac{6}{7}$. $\frac{5}{6}$ is $\frac{1}{6}$ away from 1. $\frac{6}{7}$ is $\frac{1}{7}$ away from 1. Because $\frac{1}{7} < \frac{1}{6}$, $\frac{6}{7}$ is closer to 1. So, $\frac{5}{6} < \frac{6}{7}$.

Compare.

13. $\frac{7}{8}$ ⬤ $\frac{8}{9}$

14. $\frac{2}{3}$ ⬤ $\frac{3}{7}$

15. $\frac{7}{8}$ ⬤ $\frac{6}{7}$

16. $\frac{2}{5}$ ⬤ $\frac{5}{9}$

17. $\frac{4}{5}$ ⬤ $\frac{5}{6}$

18. $\frac{7}{12}$ ⬤ $\frac{1}{3}$

► Mixed Practice

Compare.

19. $\frac{4}{5}$ ◯ $\frac{2}{3}$ 20. $\frac{9}{12}$ ◯ $\frac{6}{8}$ 21. $\frac{7}{9}$ ◯ $\frac{7}{10}$

22. $\frac{2}{3}$ ◯ $\frac{5}{6}$ 23. $\frac{5}{9}$ ◯ $\frac{3}{7}$ 24. $\frac{9}{10}$ ◯ $\frac{8}{9}$

25. $\frac{1}{5}$ ◯ $\frac{2}{9}$ 26. $\frac{3}{8}$ ◯ $\frac{1}{3}$ 27. $\frac{7}{10}$ ◯ $\frac{4}{5}$

Solve.

28. In the last basketball game, Joel made 4 out of 7 free throws. Carlos made 5 out of 9 free throws. Which boy made the greater fraction of his free throws?

Show your work on your paper or in your journal.

29. Julie lives $\frac{3}{8}$ mile from school. Madeline lives $\frac{5}{12}$ mile from school. Which girl lives closer to school?

30. Nisha and Tim are reading the same book. Nisha has finished $\frac{9}{10}$ of the book. Tim has finished $\frac{8}{9}$ of the book. Who has read more?

31. Julio's trail mix recipe has $\frac{2}{3}$ cup of almonds. Paula's trail mix recipe has $\frac{3}{4}$ cup of almonds. Whose recipe has more almonds?

32. At Coleman School, 3 out of every 7 students are in band or orchestra. At Tompkins School, 5 out of every 11 students are in band or orchestra. At which school are a greater fraction of students in band or orchestra?

► Change Mixed Numbers to Fractions

A **mixed number** is a number with a whole number part and a fraction part. For example, $2\frac{1}{2}$ is a mixed number. It means 2 *and* $\frac{1}{2}$, or 2 *plus* $\frac{1}{2}$. Mixed numbers can be rewritten as fractions.

Example: $2\frac{1}{2} = 2 + \frac{1}{2} = 1 + 1 + \frac{1}{2} = \frac{2}{2} + \frac{2}{2} + \frac{1}{2} = \frac{5}{2}$

Change each mixed number to a fraction.

1. $3\frac{2}{5} = \blacksquare$

2. $2\frac{3}{8} = \blacksquare$

3. $1\frac{7}{10} = \blacksquare$

4. $4\frac{1}{4} = \blacksquare$

5. $2\frac{5}{9} = \blacksquare$

6. $1\frac{1}{25} = \blacksquare$

► Change Fractions to Mixed Numbers

Any fraction greater than 1 can be rewritten as a mixed number.

Example: $\frac{13}{4} = \frac{4}{4} + \frac{4}{4} + \frac{4}{4} + \frac{1}{4} = 1 + 1 + 1 + \frac{1}{4} = 3\frac{1}{4}$

Change each fraction to a mixed number.

7. $\frac{10}{7} = \blacksquare$

8. $\frac{12}{5} = \blacksquare$

9. $\frac{8}{3} = \blacksquare$

10. $\frac{15}{4} = \blacksquare$

11. $\frac{39}{6} = \blacksquare$

12. $\frac{51}{10} = \blacksquare$

Show your work on your paper or in your journal.

▶ Real World Problems

13. Jonah ran around a $\frac{1}{4}$-mile track 15 times. Express the distance he ran as a mixed number.

14. A guidance counselor has $2\frac{3}{6}$ hours to meet with students. If she meets with each student for $\frac{1}{6}$ hour, how many students can she see?

▶ What's the Error?

Dear Math Students,

I had to write $3\frac{4}{5}$ as a fraction as part of my homework. I think that $3\frac{4}{5}$ means 3 four-fifths. This is what I wrote:

$3\frac{4}{5} = \frac{4}{5} + \frac{4}{5} + \frac{4}{5} = \frac{12}{5}$

My friend told me this is not correct. What did I do wrong? Can you explain how I can write $3\frac{4}{5}$ as a fraction?

Your friend,
Puzzled Penguin

15. Write a response to Puzzled Penguin.

▶ Practice Adding Mixed Numbers

Add. Write each total as a mixed number or a whole number.

1. $4\frac{1}{9} + 2\frac{1}{9}$

2. $5\frac{3}{8} + 2\frac{2}{8}$

3. $1\frac{1}{6} + 3\frac{4}{6}$

4. $4\frac{1}{3} + 6\frac{1}{3}$

5. $2\frac{1}{4} + 2\frac{3}{4}$

6. $3\frac{2}{7} + 2\frac{5}{7}$

7. $1\frac{3}{5} + 2\frac{4}{5}$

8. $40\frac{6}{7} + 22\frac{5}{7}$

9. $6\frac{8}{9} + 4\frac{7}{9}$

▶ Practice Subtracting Mixed Numbers

Subtract. Write the difference as a mixed number or a whole number.

10. $3\frac{2}{3} - 1\frac{1}{3}$

11. $5\frac{1}{6} - 3\frac{5}{6}$

12. $2\frac{3}{4} - 1\frac{3}{4}$

13. $4 - 2\frac{3}{8}$

14. $15\frac{7}{9} - 10\frac{5}{9}$

15. $12\frac{2}{5} - 8\frac{4}{5}$

▶ Solve Real World Problems

Write an equation. Then solve.

Show your work on your paper or in your journal.

16. A bag contained $6\frac{2}{3}$ cups of flour. Scout used $2\frac{1}{3}$ cups to make some bread. How much flour was left in the bag after she made the bread?

17. Tami and Ty were partners on a science project. Tami worked $4\frac{1}{4}$ hours on the project, and Ty worked $1\frac{3}{4}$ hours. How much time did they spend on the project in all?

> Show your work on your paper or in your journal.

► Solve Real World Problems (continued)

18. Maryl measures her height very precisely. Last month, she was $56\frac{7}{8}$ inches tall. This month she is $\frac{3}{8}$ inch taller. How tall is she this month?

19. Maryl (from Problem 18) measured her younger brother on January 1 of this year and found that he was $40\frac{3}{16}$ inches tall. On January 1 of last year, he was $37\frac{15}{16}$ inches tall. How much did he grow in a year's time?

► What's the Error?

Dear Math Students,

This is a problem from my math homework. My teacher says my answer is not correct, but I can't figure out what I did wrong. Can you help me find and fix my mistake?

Your friend,
Puzzled Penguin

$$5\frac{7}{5}$$
$$\cancel{5\frac{2}{5}}$$
$$-3\frac{4}{5}$$
$$\overline{2\frac{3}{5}}$$

20. Write a response to Puzzled Penguin.

Use Activity
Workbook page 8.

► Use Models to Choose a Denominator

To add two fractions, they must have a common denominator.

Use the models to help you rewrite each sum so the fractions have a common denominator. Below the model, show how to find the equivalent fractions numerically.

1.

1 whole

$\frac{1}{2} + \frac{1}{3}$

| $\frac{1}{2}$ | $\frac{1}{3}$ | |

$\boxed{} + \boxed{}$

| $\frac{1}{6}$ | $\frac{1}{6}$ | $\frac{1}{6}$ | $\frac{1}{6}$ | $\frac{1}{6}$ | |

$\dfrac{1 \times \boxed{}}{2 \times \boxed{}} = \dfrac{3}{6}$　$\dfrac{1 \times \boxed{}}{3 \times \boxed{}} = \dfrac{2}{6}$　The common denominator is _____.

2.

$\frac{1}{4} + \frac{2}{3}$

| $\frac{1}{4}$ | $\frac{1}{3}$ | $\frac{1}{3}$ | |

$\boxed{} + \boxed{}$

| $\frac{1}{12}$ | $\frac{1}{12}$ | $\frac{1}{12}$ | $\frac{1}{12}$ | $\frac{1}{12}$ | $\frac{1}{12}$ | $\frac{1}{12}$ | $\frac{1}{12}$ | $\frac{1}{12}$ | $\frac{1}{12}$ | $\frac{1}{12}$ | $\frac{1}{12}$ |

$\dfrac{1 \times \boxed{}}{4 \times \boxed{}} = \dfrac{3}{12}$　$\dfrac{2 \times \boxed{}}{3 \times \boxed{}} = \dfrac{8}{12}$　The common denominator is _____.

3.

$\frac{1}{4} + \frac{1}{2}$

| $\frac{1}{4}$ | $\frac{1}{2}$ | |

$\boxed{} + \boxed{}$

| $\frac{1}{8}$ | $\frac{1}{8}$ | $\frac{1}{8}$ | $\frac{1}{8}$ | $\frac{1}{8}$ | $\frac{1}{8}$ | $\frac{1}{8}$ | $\frac{1}{8}$ |

$\boxed{} + \boxed{}$

| $\frac{1}{4}$ | $\frac{1}{4}$ | $\frac{1}{4}$ | $\frac{1}{4}$ |

Which common denominator would you use?

Why?

4. Does $\frac{1}{2} + \frac{1}{3} = \frac{2}{5}$? _____ Discuss why or why not.

▶ Choose a Common Denominator

Rewrite the addition problem so the fractions have a common denominator. Then find the sum.

5. $\frac{7}{10} + \frac{1}{5} =$ _____ ▪ _____ = _____ ▪ _____

6. $\frac{3}{11} + \frac{1}{2} =$ _____ ▪ _____ = _____ ▪ _____

7. $\frac{1}{6} + \frac{3}{4} =$ _____ ▪ _____ = _____ ▪ _____

8. $\frac{3}{8} + \frac{2}{5} =$ _____ ▪ _____ = _____ ▪ _____

9. $\frac{3}{10} + \frac{4}{15} =$ _____ ▪ _____ = _____ ▪ _____

10. $\frac{1}{4} + \frac{5}{8} =$ _____ ▪ _____ = _____ ▪ _____

11. Bashir walked $\frac{1}{4}$ mile to his friend's house and then another $\frac{3}{8}$ mile to the park. Make a diagram to help you find the total distance he walked.

Show your work on your paper or in your journal.

Write an equation. Then solve.

12. Meg and Marcus are making a latch-hook rug. So far, Meg has finished $\frac{2}{5}$ of the rug, and Marcus has finished $\frac{1}{4}$. What fraction of the rug have they completed?

13. Of the songs downloaded from a music web site on Tuesday, $\frac{1}{6}$ were country songs and $\frac{3}{10}$ were rock songs. What fraction of the songs were country or rock songs?

Add Unlike Fractions

► Compare and Subtract

Show your work on your paper or in your journal.

Solve.

1. Amie used $\frac{7}{9}$ yard of ribbon in her dress. Jasmine used $\frac{5}{6}$ yard of ribbon in her dress.

   Which girl used more ribbon?

   How much more did she use?

2. Mr. Su and Mr. Franks are in the same book club. Mr. Su is $\frac{5}{7}$ of the way through this month's book. Mr. Franks is $\frac{3}{5}$ of the way through the book.

   Who has read more of the book?

   How much more has he read?

3. Rami's glass is $\frac{1}{2}$ full. Will's glass is $\frac{3}{8}$ full.

   Whose glass is fuller?

   How much fuller is it?

► Subtraction Practice

Subtract.

4. $\frac{1}{2} - \frac{1}{5}$

5. $\frac{3}{4} - \frac{1}{8}$

6. $\frac{9}{10} - \frac{4}{15}$

7. $\frac{1}{3} - \frac{2}{9}$

8. $\frac{5}{6} - \frac{3}{4}$

9. $\frac{3}{5} - \frac{1}{4}$

10. $\frac{4}{7} - \frac{1}{8}$

11. $\frac{5}{8} - \frac{1}{6}$

12. $\frac{11}{15} - \frac{3}{5}$

▶ Mixed Practice

Add or subtract.

13. $\frac{11}{12} - \frac{5}{12}$

14. $\frac{1}{4} + \frac{5}{12}$

15. $\frac{2}{3} - \frac{5}{9}$

16. $\frac{2}{5} + \frac{1}{3}$

17. $\frac{1}{4} - \frac{5}{32}$

18. $\frac{5}{6} - \frac{2}{9}$

19. $\frac{2}{7} + \frac{5}{7}$

20. $\frac{9}{16} - \frac{5}{24}$

21. $\frac{1}{7} - \frac{1}{8}$

Circle the greater fraction. Then write and solve a subtraction problem to find the difference of the fractions.

Show your work on your paper or in your journal.

22. $\frac{4}{5}$ $\frac{8}{9}$

23. $\frac{3}{10}$ $\frac{2}{5}$

24. $\frac{1}{6}$ $\frac{3}{20}$

Solve.

25. Bette has $\frac{2}{5}$ pound of trail mix. Johnna has $\frac{3}{8}$ pound of trail mix.

    Who has more trail mix?

    How much more does she have?

26. If Bette and Johnna from Problem 25 combine their trail mix, will they have more or less than $\frac{3}{4}$ pound? Explain.

Subtract Unlike Fractions

▶ Share Solutions

Add or subtract. Show your work.

1. $2\frac{3}{8}$
   $-1\frac{1}{4}$

2. $4\frac{1}{5}$
   $+2\frac{1}{3}$

3. $7\frac{5}{6}$
   $-3\frac{1}{4}$

4. $6\frac{2}{3}$
   $+4\frac{3}{4}$

5. $4\frac{1}{3}$
   $-2\frac{7}{15}$

6. $9\frac{1}{6}$
   $-5\frac{7}{9}$

▶ Add and Subtract Mixed Numbers

Add or subtract. Show your work.

7. $5\frac{2}{5}$
   $-3\frac{7}{10}$

8. $8\frac{1}{4}$
   $+2\frac{4}{5}$

9. $7\frac{1}{8}$
   $-4\frac{5}{12}$

10. $6\frac{8}{12}$
    $-3\frac{1}{6}$

11. $5\frac{5}{6}$
    $+2\frac{5}{9}$

12. 3
    $-1\frac{7}{11}$

13. $5\frac{5}{8}$
    $+3\frac{5}{12}$

14. $7\frac{1}{10}$
    $-2\frac{3}{5}$

15. $4\frac{1}{5}$
    $-3\frac{1}{3}$

▶ Solve Word Problems

Write an equation. Then solve.

Show your work on your paper or in your journal.

16. Dora the elephant used to eat $2\frac{3}{4}$ tons of food each month. Now she is on a diet and eats only $1\frac{7}{8}$ tons. By how many tons was Dora's food decreased each month?

17. Daisy the elephant can reach a branch $10\frac{5}{6}$ feet off the ground. Leroy, the tallest elephant, can reach a branch $1\frac{1}{2}$ feet higher than this. How high can Leroy reach?

18. Speedy, the fastest elephant, can run $25\frac{1}{10}$ miles per hour. Squirt can run only $10\frac{3}{5}$ miles per hour. How many fewer miles can Squirt run in an hour than Speedy?

Name all the possible pairs.

19. The truck that carries the elephants holds 10 tons. Which two elephants could travel together in the truck?

Dora	$5\frac{3}{4}$ tons
Leroy	$6\frac{1}{2}$ tons
Daisy	$4\frac{2}{3}$ tons
Speedy	$5\frac{2}{3}$ tons
Squirt	$3\frac{2}{3}$ tons

Solve with Unlike Mixed Numbers

► Choose How to Rename Fractions

The equations in each group have something in common.

Complete each equation.

Group 1	Group 2	Group 3

1. $\frac{9}{10} - \frac{2}{3} = \blacksquare$ 2. $\frac{9}{14} - \frac{2}{7} = \blacksquare$ 3. $\frac{5}{8} - \frac{1}{12} = \blacksquare$

4. $4\frac{3}{5} + 2\frac{3}{4} = \blacksquare$ 5. $\frac{3}{28} + \frac{3}{4} = \blacksquare$ 6. $8\frac{5}{6} - 4\frac{3}{4} = \blacksquare$

7. $\frac{2}{9} + \frac{1}{7} = \blacksquare$ 8. $3\frac{4}{18} - 1\frac{1}{3} = \blacksquare$ 9. $\frac{11}{30} + \frac{16}{45} = \blacksquare$

10. Look at the problems in Group 1.

    a. What do the problems in Group 1 have in common? (Hint: Focus on the denominators.)

    b. Describe a strategy for finding a common denominator for problems of this type.

11. Look at the problems in Group 2.

    a. What do the problems in Group 2 have in common?

    b. Describe a strategy for finding a common denominator for problems of this type.

12. Look at the problems in Group 3.

    a. What do the problems in Group 3 have in common?

    b. Describe a strategy for finding a common denominator for problems of this type.

► Practice Adding and Subtracting

Add or subtract.

13. $6\frac{3}{4} - 4\frac{1}{2}$

14. $4\frac{2}{9} + 1\frac{2}{3}$

15. $3\frac{3}{10} - 1\frac{3}{4}$

16. $2\frac{7}{8} + \frac{7}{8}$

17. $4 - 1\frac{3}{7}$

18. $1\frac{3}{5} + 1\frac{4}{7}$

19. $\frac{7}{9} + \frac{5}{6}$

20. $3\frac{1}{6} - 1\frac{1}{7}$

21. $8\frac{7}{12} + 7\frac{3}{4}$

22. $2 + \frac{1}{8} - 1\frac{1}{3}$

23. $45\frac{33}{100} + 54\frac{7}{10}$

24. $5\frac{1}{12} - 2\frac{4}{9}$

Use the line plot for Problems 25 and 26.

Every week, Mr. Park asks for 1 pound of potato salad at the deli. The line plot shows the actual weight of the salad the deli worker has given him for the past several weeks.

Weight in Pounds

25. What is the difference between the greatest and least weights shown on this graph?

26. For three of the weeks, Mr. Park received less than a pound. What is the combined weight of the salad for these three weeks?

Practice with Unlike Mixed Numbers

VOCABULARY
estimate
benchmark
round

▶ Estimate Sums and Differences

You can **estimate** the sum or difference of fractions using the **benchmarks** 0, $\frac{1}{2}$, and 1. A number line can help you determine which benchmark each fraction is closest to.

Use benchmarks of 0, $\frac{1}{2}$, and 1 to estimate the sum or difference. Then find the actual sum or difference.

1. $\frac{1}{4} + \frac{7}{8}$

   Estimate:

   Sum:

2. $\frac{7}{16} - \frac{5}{12}$

   Estimate:

   Difference:

3. $\frac{5}{6} + \frac{9}{10}$

   Estimate:

   Sum:

To estimate the sum or difference of mixed numbers, **round** each mixed number to the nearest whole number or to the nearest half.

Estimate the sum or difference by rounding each mixed number to the nearest whole number. Then find the actual sum or difference.

4. $5\frac{2}{3} - 3\frac{1}{6}$

   Estimate:

   Difference:

5. $1\frac{1}{4} + 2\frac{7}{10}$

   Estimate:

   Sum:

6. $3\frac{3}{8} - 1\frac{3}{16}$

   Estimate:

   Difference:

Use any method you wish to estimate the sum or difference.

7. $10\frac{1}{5} + 5\frac{6}{11}$

   Estimate:

   Sum:

8. $6\frac{2}{9} - 2\frac{5}{6}$

   Estimate:

   Difference:

9. $\frac{4}{7} + \frac{7}{9}$

   Estimate:

   Sum:

10. $\frac{3}{5} - \frac{4}{9}$

    Estimate:

    Difference:

11. $5\frac{1}{4} + 4\frac{1}{5}$

    Estimate:

    Sum:

12. $8\frac{4}{5} - 6\frac{1}{8}$

    Estimate:

    Difference:

► What's the Error?

Dear Math Students,

I got the two answers below marked wrong on my math test.

$3\frac{1}{4} - 1\frac{7}{8} = 2\frac{3}{8}$ $\frac{7}{8} + \frac{4}{9} = \frac{11}{17}$

My friend got 100% on the test. She said she always uses estimation to make sure her answers are reasonable.

Can you explain how I could have used estimation to check my answers?

Your friend,
Puzzled Penguin

13. Write a response to Puzzled Penguin.

► Is the Answer Reasonable?

Is the answer reasonable or unreasonable? Explain.

14. $\frac{9}{10} - \frac{2}{5} = 1\frac{3}{10}$

15. $2\frac{4}{5} + 6\frac{1}{6} = 8\frac{29}{30}$

16. $\frac{11}{12} - \frac{7}{8} = \frac{1}{24}$

17. $5\frac{5}{6} + 1\frac{3}{4} = 5\frac{1}{12}$

> Show your work on your paper or in your journal.

▶ One-Step Problems

Write an equation and solve the problem. Explain how you know your answer is reasonable.

1. Ariel ran $6\frac{1}{4}$ miles on Saturday. This is $1\frac{3}{4}$ miles more than Harry ran. How far did Harry run?

   Equation and answer:

   Why is the answer reasonable?

2. After guests drank $4\frac{1}{2}$ gallons of punch, there were $2\frac{5}{8}$ gallons left in the bowl. How much punch was in the bowl to start?

   Equation and answer:

   Why is the answer reasonable?

3. The beach is $7\frac{1}{3}$ miles from Johanna's house. She walks part of the way. Then she takes the bus the remaining $5\frac{7}{10}$ miles. How far does she walk?

   Equation and answer:

   Why is the answer reasonable?

4. At a pizza party, the Mehta family ate $1\frac{3}{8}$ pizzas in all. They ate $\frac{9}{12}$ of a cheese pizza and some pepperoni pizza. How much pepperoni pizza did they eat?

   Equation and answer:

   Why is the answer reasonable?

▶ **Problems with More Than One Step**

Show your work on your paper or in your journal.

Solve. Explain how you know your answer is reasonable.

5. Nora read $\frac{1}{6}$ of a book on Monday and $\frac{2}{5}$ on Tuesday. What fraction of the book does she have left to read?

   Answer:

   Why is the answer reasonable?

6. A rain barrel contained 32 gallons of water. Bettina used $15\frac{1}{4}$ gallons to water her garden. Then it rained, adding $6\frac{3}{4}$ more gallons. How much water is in the rain barrel now?

   Answer:

   Why is the answer reasonable?

7. Ana hikes $3\frac{7}{8}$ miles and stops for lunch. Then she hikes $5\frac{1}{4}$ more miles and stops to rest. A sign where she stops says it is $2\frac{1}{2}$ miles to the end of the trail. How long is the trail?

   Answer:

   Why is the answer reasonable?

8. A pitcher contained 8 cups of juice. The four Alvarez children drank $\frac{2}{3}$ cup, $1\frac{2}{3}$ cups, $1\frac{1}{4}$ cups, and $1\frac{3}{4}$ cups. How much juice is left?

   Answer:

   Why is the answer reasonable?

Real World Problems

▶ Math and Bird Hotels

Have you ever seen a birdhouse? Birdhouses offer birds a place to rest and keep their eggs safe from predators.

Purple martins are birds that nest in colonies. Purple martin birdhouses, like the one at the right, are sometimes called bird hotels.

Suppose that a fifth grade class has decided to build a two-story purple martin bird hotel. Each story of the hotel will have six identical compartments. One story is shown below.

The bird hotel will be made from wood, and each story will have the following characteristics.

▶ The inside dimensions of each compartment measure $7\frac{1}{2}$ in. by $7\frac{1}{2}$ in. by $7\frac{1}{2}$ in.

▶ The wood used for exterior walls is $\frac{5}{8}$-in. thick.

▶ The wood used for interior walls is $\frac{1}{4}$-in. thick.

Calculate the length, width, and height of one story. Do not include a floor or ceiling in your calculations.

1. length _____ in.

2. width _____ in.

3. height _____ in.

► Math and Bird Hotels (continued)

The bird hotel will have these additional characteristics.

► Each story has a floor that creates an overhang of 1 inch in all directions.

► The roof is flat and creates an overhang of 1 inch in all directions.

► The wood used for the floors and roof is $\frac{3}{4}$-in. thick.

Calculate the total length, width, and height of the hotel. Include floors and a roof in your calculations.

4. length _____ in.

5. width _____ in.

6. height _____ in.

Purple martins migrate great distances, spending winter in South America and summer in the United States and Canada. A diet of flying insects supplies purple martins with the energy they need to complete such long flights.

Suppose a purple martin migrates about 4,150 miles to South America each fall and about 4,150 miles back to North America each spring. Also suppose the purple martin performs this round trip once each year for three years.

7. At the Equator, the distance around Earth is about 24,900 miles. About how many times around Earth would the purple martin described above fly during its migrations?

Use the Activity Workbook Unit Test on pages 9–10.

VOCABULARY
common denominator
equivalent fractions
mixed number
unit fractions

► Vocabulary

Choose the best term from the box.

1. The number $5\frac{1}{3}$ is a _____ because it has a whole number part and a fraction part. **(Lessons 1-5)**

2. $\frac{1}{3}$ and $\frac{1}{12}$ are _____. **(Lesson 1-1)**

3. To compare $\frac{2}{5}$ and $\frac{5}{6}$, first rewrite them as equivalent fractions with a _____. **(Lesson 1-4)**

► Concepts and Skills

4. Use the fraction bar below to help you explain why $\frac{3}{4}$ and $\frac{6}{8}$ are equivalent fractions. **(Lesson 1-2)**

5. Explain how you know that the sum below is *not* reasonable without computing the actual sum. **(Lesson 1-11)**

$$\frac{8}{9} + \frac{1}{7} = \frac{35}{63}$$

Write two fractions equivalent to the given fraction. (Lessons 1-2, 1-3)

6. $\frac{5}{6}$

7. $\frac{9}{15}$

8. $\frac{2}{10}$

Compare. (Lessons 1-4)

9. $\frac{3}{10}$ ⬤ $\frac{3}{11}$

10. $\frac{5}{9}$ ⬤ $\frac{7}{12}$

11. $\frac{1}{3}$ ⬤ $\frac{3}{8}$

Add or subtract. (Lessons 1-6 through 1-10)

12. $\frac{2}{9} + \frac{2}{3}$

13. $\frac{5}{8} - \frac{3}{10}$

14. $7\frac{1}{5} - 1\frac{2}{3}$

15. $\frac{6}{7} + 2\frac{5}{6}$

16. $4\frac{1}{5} - 3\frac{7}{10}$

17. $1\frac{5}{8} + 2\frac{1}{2}$

▶ Problem Solving

Write an equation. Then solve. (Lessons 1-7 through 1-13)

18. Zora left late for soccer practice, so she ran the first $\frac{5}{8}$ mile. Then she got tired and had to walk the remaining $\frac{7}{10}$ mile. How far was it from Zora's home to practice?

19. Scott has $2\frac{3}{4}$ cups of flour. He wants to make a muffin recipe that calls for $4\frac{1}{3}$ cups of flour. How much more flour does he need?

20. **Extended Response** Jen bought $5\frac{1}{4}$ yards of blue fabric and $3\frac{2}{3}$ yards of red fabric. She gave $2\frac{3}{4}$ yards of fabric to her cousin. How much fabric does she have left? Explain how you know your answer is reasonable.

Dear Family,

Your child has studied addition and subtraction with whole numbers and decimals in past years. Unit 2 of *Math Expressions* guides students as they study these topics in greater depth.

The main goals of this unit are:

1. to help students extend their understanding of place value for decimals;

2. to help students add and subtract decimals using the methods they learned previously to add and subtract whole numbers;

3. to develop rounding skills as students estimate sums and differences and engage in graphing activities.

Students will extend and apply their knowledge of place value as they complete activities involving money and metric lengths. When the opportunity arises, ask your child questions about money amounts to help reinforce what is being taught in class.

Share with your family the Family Letter on Activity Workbook page 11.

To accomplish the second goal, students will use various methods of grouping. Students may use whatever method they prefer as long as they understand why it works and can explain it. To add and subtract accurately, students need to align the digits by place value correctly. Observe your child as he or she adds and subtracts. Help align the digits when necessary.

The third goal is accomplished in several ways. Students will learn to use the scale on a graph to understand how to round a number. For example, they see that a number such as 3,879 is between 3,000 and 4,000, but closer to 4,000. So, 3,879 rounded to the nearest thousand is 4,000.

Finally, students will solve real world problems that require estimating sums and differences while adding and subtracting large numbers and decimals.

If you have any questions or comments, please call or write to me.

Sincerely,
Your child's teacher

COMMON CORE

This unit includes the Common Core Standards for Mathematical Content for the Number System, CC.5.NBT.1, CC.5.NBT.3, CC.5.NBT.3a, CC.5.NBT.3b, CC.5.NBT.4, CC.5.NBT.7 and all Mathematical Practices.

Estimada familia:

Su niño ha estudiado la suma y resta de números enteros y decimales en años pasados. La Unidad 2 de *Math Expressions* guiará a los estudiantes a medida que estudien esos temas más profundamente.

Los objetivos principales de esta unidad son:

1. ayudar a los estudiantes a ampliar su comprensión del valor posicional de los decimales;

2. ayudar a los estudiantes con la suma y resta de decimales usando los métodos que aprendieron anteriormente para sumar y restar números enteros;

3. desarrollar destrezas de redondeo al estimar sumas y restas y hacer actividades con gráficas.

Los estudiantes ampliarán y aplicarán su conocimiento del valor posicional al realizar actividades con dinero y medidas métricas. Cuando se presente la ocasión, hágale preguntas a su niño sobre cantidades de dinero para reforzar lo que se enseña en la clase.

Los estudiantes lograrán el segundo objetivo utilizando varios métodos de agrupación. Pueden usar el método que prefieran, mientras comprendan por qué funciona y puedan explicarlo. Para sumar y restar con exactitud, necesitan alinear correctamente los dígitos según el valor posicional. Observe a su niño mientras suma y resta. Ayúdele a alinear los dígitos cuando haga falta.

El tercer objetivo se puede cumplir de varias maneras. Los estudiantes aprenderán a usar la escala de una gráfica para comprender cómo se redondea un número. Por ejemplo, van a ver que un número como 3,879 está entre 3,000 y 4,000, pero está más cerca de 4,000. Por lo tanto, redondear 3,879 al millar más cercano da 4,000.

Finalmente, los estudiantes resolverán problemas cotidianos que requieran estimar sumas y restas al sumar y restar números grandes y decimales.

Si tiene alguna pregunta o algún comentario, por favor comuníquese conmigo.

Atentamente,
El maestro de su niño

> Muestra a tu familia la Carta a la familia de la página 12 del Cuaderno de actividades y trabajo.

COMMON CORE Esta unidad incluye los Common Core Standards for Mathematical Content for the Number System, CC.5.NBT.1, CC.5.NBT.3, CC.5.NBT.3a, CC.5.NBT.3b, CC.5.NBT.4, CC.5.NBT.7 and all Mathematical Practices.

VOCABULARY
decimal
tenth
hundredth
thousandth

▶ Discuss Fractions and Decimals

Fractions and decimals are special kinds of numbers. They
tell the number of equal parts a whole is divided into, and
the number of those parts that are being taken or described.

Fraction notation uses a numerator and a denominator
to show a whole divided into any number of equal parts.

1.

1 Whole

4 equal parts

$\frac{1}{4}$ + $\frac{1}{4}$ + $\frac{1}{4}$ + $\frac{1}{4}$

1 part $\frac{1}{4}$
1 of 4 equal parts

2.

1 Whole

5 equal parts

$\frac{1}{5}$ + $\frac{1}{5}$ + $\frac{1}{5}$ + $\frac{1}{5}$ + $\frac{1}{5}$

3 parts $\frac{3}{5}$
3 of 5 equal parts

Decimal notation uses a decimal point to show places to the
right of the ones place. The **tenths** place shows 1 whole
(such as one dollar) divided into 10 equal parts. The **hundredths**
place shows each tenth divided into 10 equal parts.

3.

$\frac{1}{10}$ 1 of 10 equal parts

$ 0.10   one dime or one tenth of a dollar

0.1   1 in the tenths place

4.

$\frac{1}{100}$ 1 of 100 equal parts

$0.01   one penny or one hundredth of a dollar

0.01   1 in the hundredths place

The **thousandths** place shows each hundredth divided into 10 equal parts.

5.

$\frac{1}{10}$
of a penny

$\frac{1}{1,000}$ 1 of 1,000 equal parts

$0.001   one tenth of penny or one thousandth of a dollar

0.001   1 in the thousandths place

▶ Decimals as Equal Parts of Sets

Decimal numbers are read as if they are fractions.
$\frac{37}{100}$ and 0.37 are both said as *thirty-seven hundredths*.

Write each fraction as a decimal number, and then say the number.

6. $\frac{7}{100}$ 　　　　7. $\frac{16}{100}$ 　　　　8. $\frac{4}{10}$ 　　　　9. $\frac{9}{10}$

10. $\frac{5}{1,000}$ 　　　11. $\frac{54}{1,000}$ 　　　12. $\frac{81}{100}$ 　　　13. $\frac{409}{1,000}$

14. $\frac{2}{10}$ 　　　　15. $\frac{3}{100}$ 　　　　16. $\frac{16}{1,000}$ 　　　17. $\frac{67}{100}$

18. Discuss the patterns you can see in the exercises above. Then explain how to say any decimal number.

Solve.

19. If you cut a lemon into 10 equal pieces, what decimal number would 3 pieces represent?

20. A bag of pretzels contains 100 pretzels. What decimal number would 28 pretzels represent? What decimal number would 5 pretzels represent?

21. A beehive is home to 1,000 bees. If 235 bees are out gathering pollen, what decimal number do those bees represent?

22. What decimal number is represented by answering 92 of 100 test questions correctly?

Use Activity Workbook page 13.

▶ Place Value Chart

Discuss the patterns you see in the Place Value Chart below.

◀ × 10 (Larger)   **Place Value Chart**   ÷ 10 (Smaller) ▶

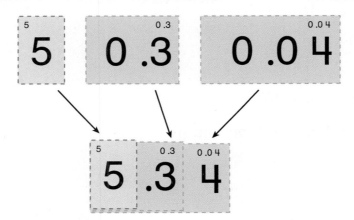

Thousands	Hundreds	Tens	ONES	Tenths	Hundredths	Thousandths
1,000.	100.	10.	1.	0.1	0.01	0.001
$\frac{1,000}{1}$	$\frac{100}{1}$	$\frac{10}{1}$	$\frac{1}{1}$	$\frac{1}{10}$	$\frac{1}{100}$	$\frac{1}{1,000}$
$1,000.00	$100.00	$10.00	$1	$0.10	$0.01	$0.001

5   **5**   0.3   **0 .3**   0.04   **0.0 4**

5   0.3   0.04   **5 .3 4**

Use your Secret-Code Cards to make numbers on the frame.

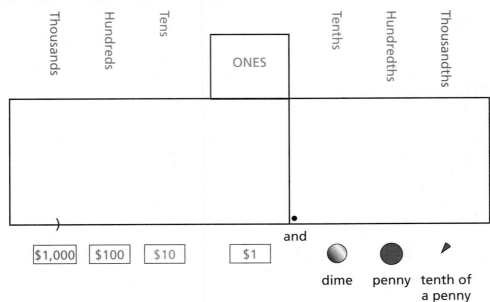

and

$1,000 $100 $10 $1   dime   penny   tenth of a penny

Use Activity
Workbook page 14.

▶ Represent Numbers Different Ways

In our place value system, numbers can be expressed different ways. For example, four different ways to represent the number 35.026 are shown below.

standard form	35.026
word form	thirty-five and twenty-six thousandths
expanded form	$30 + 5 + 0.02 + 0.006$
expanded form (powers of 10)	$(3 \times 10) + (5 \times 1) + (2 \times \frac{1}{100}) + (6 \times \frac{1}{1,000})$

Write each number in three different ways.

1. 12,402

   word form

   expanded form

   expanded form (powers of 10)

2. eight and three hundred five thousandths

   standard form

   expanded form

   expanded form (powers of 10)

3. $70 + 2 + 0.4 + 0.03$

   standard form

   expanded form (powers of 10)

   word form

4. $(4 \times 10,000) + (2 \times 1,000) + (3 \times 10) + (5 \times 1) + (2 \times \frac{1}{10}) + (2 \times \frac{1}{1,000})$

   standard form

   word form

   expanded form

Thousands to Thousandths

Use Activity Workbook page 21.

VOCABULARY
equivalent decimals

▶ Visualize with Other Models

1. The bar below represents one whole or 1.

a. Shade 6 tenths and then shade 2 hundredths.

b. **Discuss** Why does the drawing show 0.6 + 0.02 = 0.60 + 0.02 = 0.62?

2. The number line below is labeled by tenths from 0 to 1.

```
 ←—+——+——+——+——+——+——+——+——+——+——+→
   0  0.1  0.2  0.3  0.4  0.5  0.6  0.7  0.8  0.9  1.0
```

a. Begin at 0 and circle a distance to show 0.28 = 0.2 + 0.08 = 0.20 + 0.08.

b. Circle a new distance to show 0.74 = 0.7 + 0.04 = 0.70 + 0.04.

3. Shade the grids to show each amount.

a. 0.4 = 0.40   **b.** 0.36 = 0.3 + 0.06   **c.** 0.001

4. Use a sketch of money, a bar representing one whole, a number line, or one or more grids to prove that each statement below is true.

a. 0.3 = 0.30   **b.** 0.070 = 0.07

5. **Discuss** **Equivalent decimals** represent the same value. Why does writing zeros to the right of a decimal number not change the value of the number?

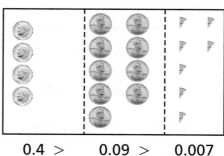

Use Activity Workbook page 22.

▶ Practice Comparisons

We can use Secret-Code Cards to compare decimal numbers.
For example, these cards show that 0.4 > 0.09 and 0.09 > 0.007.

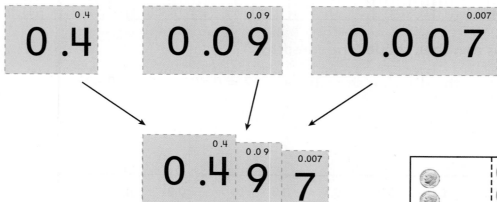

We can also use dimes to represent tenths and pennies to represent hundredths to show that the value of a dime is greater than the value of a penny and the value of a penny is greater than the value of a tenth of a penny.

0.4 > 0.09 > 0.007

Choose any method and use it to complete the following comparisons. Write >, <, or =.

6. 0.7 ⬤ 0.700   7. 0.070 ⬤ 0.07   8. 0.07 ⬤ 0.7   9. 0.007 ⬤ 0.7

10. 0.8 ⬤ 0.62   11. 0.06 ⬤ 0.3   12. 0.475 ⬤ 0.62   13. 0.3 ⬤ 0.29

14. 0.38 ⬤ 0.038   15. 0.4 ⬤ 0.38   16. 0.38 ⬤ 0.380   17. 0.7 ⬤ 0.71

18. 0.50 ⬤ 0.5   19. 0.21 ⬤ 0.2   20. 0.111 ⬤ 0.11   21. 0.4 ⬤ 0.404

22. Describe a method for comparing decimal numbers.

Use Activity
Workbook page 23.

VOCABULARY
meter (m)
decimeter (dm)
centimeter (cm)
millimeter (mm)

▶ Explore Metric Measures of Length

Use your paper ruler to answer each question.

1. How many decimeters equal one meter?

2. How many millimeters equal one centimeter?

3. How many millimeters equal one decimeter?

4. How many millimeters equal one meter?

5. How many centimeters equal one decimeter?

6. How many centimeters equal one meter?

The last row of the Place Value Chart shows metric measures of length. The most common measurement units are **meter** (m), **decimeter** (dm), **centimeter** (cm), and **millimeter** (mm).

7. Use the meaning of *deci* (one tenth), *centi* (one hundredth), and *milli* (one thousandth) to fill in the right hand side of the chart below.

8. Use the meaning of the Greek words *kilo* (thousand), *hecto* (hundred), and *deka* (ten) to fill in the left side of the chart.

◀ **× 10 (Larger)**　　　　**Place Value Chart**　　　　**÷ 10 (Smaller)** ▶

Thousands	Hundreds	Tens	ONES	Tenths	Hundredths	Thousandths
1,000.	100.	10.	1.	0.1	0.01	0.001
$\frac{1,000}{1}$	$\frac{100}{1}$	$\frac{10}{1}$	$\frac{1}{1}$	$\frac{1}{10}$	$\frac{1}{100}$	$\frac{1}{1,000}$
$1,000.00	$100.00	$10.00	$1.00	$0.10	$0.01	$0.001
____ m kilometer km	____ m hectometer hm	____ m dekameter dam	____ meter m	____ m decimeter dm	____ m centimeter cm	____ m millimeter mm

► Real World Problems with Metric Lengths

Read each measurement below. Say the number of meters, decimeters, centimeters, and millimeters.

For example, 7.284 m is 7 meters, 2 decimeters, 8 centimeters, and 4 millimeters.

9. 7.284 m   **10.** 45.132 m   **11.** 29.16 m   **12.** 304 m   **13.** 16.02 m

Write an equation. Then solve

14. Tori had fabric that was 6.2 meters long. She used some and now has 1.45 meters. How much did she use?

Show your work on your paper or in your journal.

15. Matt is competing in the long jump event. His first jump was 3.56 m. So far, the longest jump in the event is 4.02 m. How much farther must Matt jump to be in first place?

16. Patrick ran 53 meters away from Marty and then ran 16.02 meters directly back towards him. How far was Patrick from Marty then?

17. Sarita has some ribbon. After she used 23.8 cm of it, she had 50 cm left. How much ribbon did Sarita start with?

Write your own problems.

18. Write an addition word problem using the measurements in Exercises 11 and 13.

▶ Addition Problems

When adding, remember to align the place values of the numbers.

> Dear Math Students,
>
> I am ordering a CD from a catalog. The price of the CD is $15 and the tax is $0.15. Altogether, then, I will have to pay $30 for this CD. The tax makes the cost twice as much! Doesn't this seem unreasonable to you? Or have I made some kind of a mistake?
>
> Your friend,
> Puzzled Penguin

1. Write a response to Puzzled Penguin.

Add. Try to solve mentally.

2. $28 + 32¢ = ▨

3. $42.05 + 63¢ = ▨

4. 56¢ + $8.27 = ▨

5. 43 + 0.26 = ▨

6. 57.3 + 0.89 = ▨

7. 92.17 + 1.6 = ▨

8. 4 m + 0.03 m = ▨

9. 2.5 m + 0.08 m = ▨

10. 6 m + 0.007 m = ▨

11. Explain how to add two decimal numbers. Give an example.

▶ Practice

Add each pair of numbers.

12.   4.78
    + 5.23

13. 37.56
    + 2.78

14.   203.05
    + 48.9

15. $8.59
    + $0.78

16. 9.53 + 0.7

17. 605.4 + 0.89

18. 0.37 + 0.15

19. 91 + 0.51

20.   876.2
   + 5,274.2

21. 95,238.77
   +   78.41

22. 332.28
  + 91.36

23.   66,488.82
  + 124,507.09

Write an equation. Then solve.

Show your work on your paper or in your journal.

24. When Bill got his kitten, Missy, she weighed 807.39 grams. She now weighs 1,918.7 grams more than she did when Bill first brought her home. How much does Missy weigh now?

25. Ajit is tracking how much rainfall falls at his house. The first day 1.45 centimeters of rain fell. The second day 2.3 centimeters of rain fell. On the third day, 1.68 centimeters of rain fell. How many centimeters of rain fell in all over the three days?

26. Walt is running for exercise. He ran around Lake Blue and then ran 2.75 miles home. He ran for a total of 4.25 miles. How far did he run around Lake Blue?

Add Whole Numbers and Decimals

► Subtraction with Ungrouping

Ungrouping allows you to subtract greater numbers from lesser numbers.

Dear Math Students,

I measured the depth of the snow on my iceberg and it was 40.15 cm deep. Last week the snow was 36.84 cm deep. I subtracted to find out how much it had changed and got a difference of 14.31 cm. That isn't what the meteorologist said. Can you help me find my mistake?

Your friend,
Puzzled Penguin

1. Write a response to Puzzled Penguin.

► Practice

Subtract. Use addition to check your answers.

2. 168.75
      − 59.82

3. 6,222.01
    − 48.04

4. 1.09
      − 0.7

5. 100,561.78 − 814.99

6. 0.91 − 0.88

7. 37,000 − 2.73

8. 80,615 − 74,468.63

9. 610,716 − 9.45

10. 909, 015.5 − 90,901.55

> ## Real World Problems

Write an equation. Then solve.

Show your work on your paper or in your journal.

11. One year, the Sahara Desert received 0.79 inches of rain. That same year the rain forest in Brazil received 324 inches. How much more rain fell in the rain forest that year than in the desert?

12. A newborn kangaroo measures about 0.02 meter in height. If the newborn kangaroo grows to be an adult that is 2.7 meters tall, how much will the baby kangaroo have grown?

> ## Practice

Add or subtract.

13. $\begin{array}{r} 2,333.56 \\ + 81.09 \\ \hline \end{array}$

14. $\begin{array}{r} 0.08 \\ + 0.97 \\ \hline \end{array}$

15. $\begin{array}{r} 610,877.50 \\ - 22,948 \\ \hline \end{array}$

16. $\begin{array}{r} 24 \\ - 0.18 \\ \hline \end{array}$

17. $\begin{array}{r} 555,222 \\ + 178,109.50 \\ \hline \end{array}$

18. $\begin{array}{r} 9.28 \\ + 1.76 \\ \hline \end{array}$

19. $90.44 - 1.37$

20. $4,822 - 0.08$

21. $667,087.6 + 4,055.75$

22. $807 + 3.48$

23. $77.08 - 25$

24. $2,004 - 5.43$

VOCABULARY
Commutative Property of Addition
Associative Property of Addition

▶ Practice with Regrouping and Reordering

The **Commutative Property** and **Associative Property**
can help you add.

Properties

Commutative Property of Addition $a + b = b + a$

Associative Property of Addition $(a + b) + c = a + (b + c)$

You can sometimes group or reorder numbers to help you use
mental math more quickly. Explain how you could use the
Commutative and Associative Properties to help you add mentally.

1. 30,000
    20,000
    80,000
    49,000
  + 70,000

2. 1.500
    1.200
    1.300
  + 1.678

3. 5.75
    5.4
    5.25
    5.17
  + 5.6

4. $\frac{1}{6}$
    $\frac{5}{11}$
    $\frac{3}{4}$
    $\frac{5}{6}$
  + $\frac{1}{4}$

5. 8 million + 39 million + 2 million

6. 40 hundredths + 8 and 56 hundredths + 60 hundredths

7. $\frac{8}{9} + 5\frac{1}{5} + \frac{1}{9}$

VOCABULARY
Distributative Property of Multiplication over Addition

The **Distributive Property** can also help you compute mentally.

Distributive Property	$a \times (b + c) = (a \times b) + (a \times c)$

Discuss how you could use the Distributive Property to write each problem with only two factors. Then solve the problems mentally.

8. $(7 \times 25) + (7 \times 75) = $ ■

9. $(800 \times 9) + (200 \times 9) = $ ■

10. Use what you know about the Commutative Property to solve for n.
$968.73 + 532.15 = 532.15 + n$

Find each answer by using the Associative Property.

11. $(749 + 600) + 400 = $ ■

12. $3.20 + (2.80 + 1.37) = $ ■

13. Use the Distributive Property to help you find the combined area of these rectangles.

199 cm
10 cm

101 cm
10 cm

▶ Properties and Real World Situations

Which property best describes each situation below: Commutative, Associative, or Distributive?

14. Miranda cannot add ($56.73 + $8.00) + $2.00 very easily. So, she regroups the problem as $56.73 + ($8.00 + $2.00).

15. Brady did not know the answer to 2×403. So, he broke a factor into two addends and multiplied each addend by the other factor. Then, he added the two products together: $(2 \times 400) + (2 \times 3)$.

► Round Decimal Numbers

Solve.

1. A number changed to 12.6 after it was rounded. To what place was the number rounded? Explain how you know.

2. A number changed to 3.25 after it was rounded. To what place was the number rounded? Explain how you know.

3. A number changed to 193 after it was rounded. To what place was the number rounded? Explain how you know.

Round to the nearest whole number.

4. 31.75	5. 6.49	6. 11.5
7. 0.97	8. 319.1	9. 9.086

Round to the nearest hundredth.

10. 4.051	11. 16.686	12. 0.994
13. 51.202	14. 775.115	15. 4,258.999

Round to the nearest tenth.

16. 51.16	17. 8.55	18. 147.67
19. 0.84	20. 29.20	21. 0.182

► Estimate Sums and Differences

Estimate each sum or difference.

22.	$17.25 − $11.79	23.	$8.90 + $5.80	24.	$3.52 − $1.54

25.	$6.36 + $6.81	26.	0.716 − 0.698	27.	10.239 + 9.062

Solve.

28. Rick thinks the total cost of a $89.95 soccer goal and a $9.99 soccer ball is $90.94. Write your estimate of the total cost; then write the exact cost.

Show your work on your paper or in your journal.

   Estimate   Exact Cost

   Was Rick's answer reasonable? Explain why or why not.

29. Marti has 20.15 m of red and blue fabric. Of that, 9.28 m is red, the rest is blue. Marti calculated that she has 10.87 m of blue fabric.

   Is Marti's answer reasonable? Explain why or why not.

30. In a video racing game, Lee completed one lap in 47.32 seconds. Donna completed one lap in 45.41 seconds.

   Which lap was faster?

   How many seconds faster was the lap?

   Estimate   Exact Answer

   Is your exact answer reasonable? Explain why or why not.

▶ Graphs with Decimal Numbers

This bar graph shows the length of some common beetles.

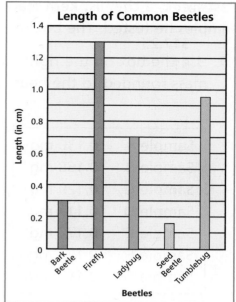

1. What is the length of a bark beetle?

2. How much longer is a firefly than a bark beetle?

3. Estimate the length of a tumblebug in hundredths of a centimeter.

4. The actual length of one beetle shown is 0.150 centimeters. Which beetle is that?

5. A June bug is about 2.5 centimeters in length. About how many times as tall as the tumblebug bar would the June bug bar be? (Hint: Round the lengths to whole numbers to help you estimate the height of the June bug's bar.)

▶ What's the Error?

Dear Math Students,

For the Science Fair, I recorded the heights of several plants a month after I put different fertilizers on them. I made a bar graph of the data. Did I make my graph correctly? If not, how can I fix it?

Your friend,
Puzzled Penguin

6. Write an answer to Puzzled Penguin.

Use Activity
Workbook page 24.

▶ **Make a Bar Graph with Decimal Numbers**

Last week, a chemist kept track of the masses of the different
samples he tested. The box on the left shows the information.

7. Use the box on the right to make a list that shows each
   mass rounded to the nearest hundredth of a milligram.

Sample A	0.136 mg
Sample B	0.168 mg
Sample C	0.129 mg
Sample D	0.117 mg
Sample E	0.179 mg
Sample F	0.162 mg
Sample G	0.109 mg

Sample A	
Sample B	
Sample C	
Sample D	
Sample E	
Sample F	
Sample G	

8. Which sample had the greatest mass?

9. Which sample had the least mass?

10. Estimate the total mass of the samples to the nearest tenth.

11. Make a bar graph to show these masses rounded
    to the nearest hundredth.

12. Write the samples' masses in order from from least to greatest.

▶ Math and Our Solar System

To describe distances on Earth, you do not need to use units of measure greater than thousands of miles. In space, however, distances are vast, and greater units of measure are used to describe those distances.

Distances between objects in our solar system usually involve many millions of miles.

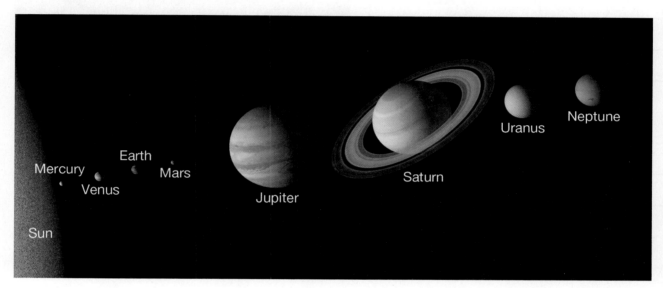

Scientists express the distances in astronomical units (AU). One AU is the distance from the Earth to our Sun, which is about 93 million miles.

$$1 \text{ AU} \approx 93{,}000{,}000 \text{ miles}$$

When you work with distances in our solar system, it is easier to add and subtract astronomical units than it is to add and subtract numbers in the millions.

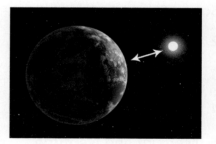

1 AU

Solve.

1. Venus orbits 0.72 AU from the Sun. Mercury's orbit is 0.33 AU closer. Explain why subtraction is used to find the distance of Mercury's orbit from the Sun. Then find the distance.

The table below shows the distances in astronomical
units (AU) of the planets from our Sun. Since the planets Mercury
and Venus are closer to the Sun than Earth, their distance
from the Sun is less than 1 AU. Outer planets such as Jupiter
and Neptune have distances greater than 1 AU.

Planet	Orbital Distance from the Sun (in AU)
Mercury	0.39
Venus	0.72
Earth	1.0
Mars	1.5
Jupiter	5.2
Saturn	9.5
Uranus	19.2
Neptune	30.1

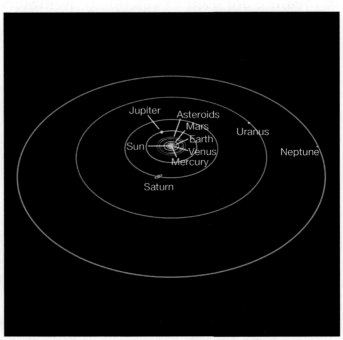

Solve. Compute the distance between the planets' orbits.

2. Venus and Earth _____ AU

3. Earth and Mars _____ AU

4. Jupiter and Saturn _____ AU

5. Mercury and Neptune _____ AU

Show your work on your paper or in your journal.

6. Write Mercury's orbital distance (in AU) from the Sun as a fraction.

7. The sum of the orbital distances from the Sun of which four planets is closest to the orbital distance from the Sun to Neptune?

Focus on Mathematical Practices

Use the Activity Workbook Unit Test on pages 25–26.

▶ Vocabulary

Choose the best term from the box.

1. The _____ shows that 2 + 8 = 2(1 + 4). **(Lessons 2-7)**

2. The _____ for the number 3.15 is the expression 3 + 0.1 + 0.05. **(Lessons 2-2)**

▶ Concepts and Skills

3. How do the values of the digit 2 in the number 222.222 change for each place value. **(Lesson 2-2)**

4. How can you use the properties to add 2.4 + 5.7 + 2.6 mentally? **(Lesson 2-7)**

5. How do you know whether to ungroup in the problem 3.42 − 1.51? **(Lesson 2-6)**

Write each number in another form. (Lessons 2-1, 2-2)

6. twenty-three thousand and four hundred six thousandths in standard form:

7. 7.42 in word form:

8. 98.704 in expanded form using powers of ten:

9. $(4 \times 10) + (5 \times 1) + (9 \times \frac{1}{100}) +$ $(3 \times \frac{1}{1,000})$ in standard form:

10. Which is greater, the value of the digit 8 in 7.819 or the value of the digit 8 in 208?

11. Which of these numbers shows the digit 3 with a value of 3 hundredths? 1.063, 2.357, or 5.234

Compare. Write <, >, or =. (Lesson 2-3)

12. 0.18 1.121　　13. 0.050 0.5　　14. 1.09 1.090　　15. 5.508 0.859

Round to the indicated place value. (Lesson 2-8, 2-9)

16. Round 40.823 to the nearest whole number.

17. Round 5.099 to the nearest hundredth.

18. Round 82.128 to the nearest tenth.

Add or subtract. (Lessons 2-4, 2-5, 2-6, 2-7)

19. 554.09
    + 36.99

20. 4.72
    − 3.89

21. 12.87
    + 0.78

22. 23.09
    − 7.53

▶ Problem Solving

Solve. Explain how you know your answer is reasonable.
(Lessons 2-4, 2-5, 2-6, 2-7, 2-8)

23. Randy caught a fish that weighed 3.53 kilograms. His brother caught a fish that weighed 5.08 kilograms. How many kilograms of fish did the boys bring home together?

24. Shasha is saving for a bicycle. Last month, Shasha saved $56.93. Last week, she received $22.50 for walking the neighbor's dog and she spent $15.76 on a CD. If the bike costs $109.99, how much more does she need to save?

25. **Extended Response** In 1931, Chuhei Nambu set a world record by jumping 7.98 meters in the long jump. In 1935, Jesse Owens set a new world record by jumping 8.13 meters.

    a. Estimate how much farther Jesse Owens jumped than Chuhei Nambu. Explain how you got your answer.

    b. Exactly how many meters farther did Jesse Owens jump?

Dear Family,

In this unit of *Math Expressions*, your child is studying multiplication and division with fractions.

Multiplication tells how many times we are taking a number. For example, when we take $\frac{4}{5}$ of something, we multiply it by $\frac{4}{5}$ to find the answer. In this unit, your child will learn to:

- multiply a whole number by a unit fraction

$$\frac{1}{b} \cdot w = \frac{w}{b} \qquad \frac{1}{3} \cdot 5 = \frac{5}{3}$$

- multiply a whole number by a non-unit fraction

$$\frac{a}{b} \cdot w = \frac{a \cdot w}{b} \qquad \frac{2}{3} \cdot 5 = \frac{10}{3}$$

- multiply two fractions

$$\frac{a}{b} \cdot \frac{c}{d} = \frac{a \cdot c}{b \cdot d} \qquad \frac{2}{3} \cdot \frac{5}{7} = \frac{10}{21}$$

Division tells us how many of a certain number are inside another number. For example, when we ask how many times $\frac{1}{5}$ fits inside a number, we divide it by $\frac{1}{5}$ to find out. Using the relationship between multiplication and division, your child will discover how to:

> *Share with your family the Family Letter on Activity Workbook page 27.*

- divide a whole number by a whole number

$$a \div b = a \cdot \frac{1}{b} = \frac{a}{b} \qquad 3 \div 4 = 3 \cdot \frac{1}{4} = \frac{3}{4}$$

- divide a whole number by a unit fraction

$$w \div \frac{1}{d} = w \cdot d \qquad 6 \div \frac{1}{5} = 6 \cdot 5 = 30$$

- divide a unit fraction by a whole number

$$\frac{1}{d} \div w = \frac{1}{d} \cdot \frac{1}{w} \qquad \frac{1}{2} \div 4 = \frac{1}{2} \cdot \frac{1}{4} = \frac{1}{8}$$

Throughout the unit, students will also practice comparing, adding, and subtracting fractions. This helps them maintain what they have learned. It also helps them to see how the various fractional operations are alike and how they are different. It is particularly important for your child to realize that comparing, adding, and subtracting fractions require the denominators to be the same. For multiplying and dividing, this is not true.

If you have any questions about this unit, please call or write to me.

Sincerely,
Your child's teacher

COMMON CORE

This unit includes the Common Core Standards for Mathematical Content for Number and Operation—Fractions, 5.NF.3, 5.NF.4, 5.NF.4a, 5.NF.4b, 5.NF.5, 5.NF.5a, 5.NF.5b, 5.NF.6, 5.NF.7, 5.NF.7a, 5.NF.7b, 5.NF.7c, and all Mathematical Practices.

Estimada familia:

En esta unidad de *Math Expressions* su niño está estudiando la multiplicación y la división con fracciones.

La multiplicación nos dice cuántas veces se toma un número. Por ejemplo, cuando tomamos $\frac{4}{5}$ de algo, lo multiplicamos por $\frac{4}{5}$ para hallar la respuesta. En esta unidad su niño aprenderá a:

- multiplicar un número entero por una fracción unitaria

$$\frac{1}{b} \cdot w = \frac{w}{b} \qquad \frac{1}{3} \cdot 5 = \frac{5}{3}$$

- multiplicar un número entero por una fracción no unitaria

$$\frac{a}{b} \cdot w = \frac{a \cdot w}{b} \qquad \frac{2}{3} \cdot 5 = \frac{10}{3}$$

- multiplicar dos fracciones

$$\frac{a}{b} \cdot \frac{c}{d} = \frac{a \cdot c}{b \cdot d} \qquad \frac{2}{3} \cdot \frac{5}{7} = \frac{10}{21}$$

La división nos dice cuántas veces cabe un número dentro de otro número. Por ejemplo, cuando preguntamos cuántas veces cabe $\frac{1}{5}$ en un número, dividimos el número entre $\frac{1}{5}$ para saberlo. Al usar la relación entre la multiplicación y la división, su niño va a descubrir cómo:

> *Muestra a tu familia la Carta a la familia de la página 28 del Cuaderno de actividades y trabajo.*

- dividir un entero entre un entero

$$a \div b = a \cdot \frac{1}{b} = \frac{a}{b} \qquad 3 \div 4 = 3 \cdot \frac{1}{4} = \frac{3}{4}$$

- dividir un entero entre una fracción unitaria

$$w \div \frac{1}{d} = w \times d \qquad 6 \div \frac{1}{5} = 6 \times 5 = 30$$

- dividir una fracción unitaria entre un entero

$$\frac{1}{d} \div w = \frac{1}{d} \times \frac{1}{w} \qquad \frac{1}{2} \div 4 = \frac{1}{2} \times \frac{1}{4} = \frac{1}{8}$$

En esta unidad los estudiantes también practicarán comparaciones, y sumas y restas con fracciones. Esto los ayudará a retener lo que han aprendido. También los ayudará a ver las semejanzas y diferencias entre las operaciones con fracciones. Es importante que su niño se dé cuenta de que para comparar, sumar y restar fracciones, las fracciones deben tener el mismo denominador. Esto no aplica para la multiplicación y división.

Si tiene alguna duda o algún comentario, por favor comuníquese conmigo.

Atentamente,
El maestro de su niño

 COMMON CORE

Esta unidad incluye los Common Core Standards for Mathematical Content for Number and Operation—Fractions, 5.NF.3, 5.NF.4, 5.NF.4a, 5.NF.4b, 5.NF.5, 5.NF.5a, 5.NF.5b, 5.NF.6, 5.NF.7, 5.NF.7a, 5.NF.7b, 5.NF.7c, and all Mathematical Practices.

Use Activity Workbook page 29.

▶ Multiply by a Unit Fraction

Complete.

1. A path around a large park is 8 kilometers long. Alex ran around the path 4 times.

   8 taken 4 times = _____ kilometers

   $4 \cdot 8 =$ _____ kilometers

2. Kento ran around the same path $\frac{1}{4}$ time.

   8 taken $\frac{1}{4}$ time = _____ kilometers

   $\frac{1}{4} \cdot 8 =$ _____ kilometers

3. Markers come in boxes of 6. Alta has 3 boxes.

   6 taken 3 times = _____ markers

   $3 \cdot 6 =$ _____ markers

3 groups of 6

4. Isabel has $\frac{1}{3}$ of a box of 6 markers.

   6 taken $\frac{1}{3}$ time = _____ markers

   $\frac{1}{3} \cdot 6 =$ _____ markers

$\frac{1}{3}$ **group of 6**

▶ Relate Fraction Multiplication and Whole Number Division

Complete each equation chain like the one shown.

$\frac{1}{4}$ of 8 $= \frac{1}{4} \cdot 8 = 8 \div 4 = \frac{8}{4} = 2$

5. $\frac{1}{3}$ of 9 $=$ _____ $=$ _____ $=$ _____ $=$ _____

6. $\frac{1}{7}$ of 21 $=$ _____ $=$ _____ $=$ _____ $=$ _____

7. $\frac{1}{5}$ of 30 $=$ _____ $=$ _____ $=$ _____ $=$ _____

8. Which expression does *not* mean the same thing as the others?

   $\frac{1}{6} \cdot 24 \qquad 24 \div 6 \qquad \frac{24}{6} \qquad \frac{6}{24} \qquad \frac{1}{6}$ of 24

VOCABULARY
comparison bars

▶ Discuss Comparison Problems

To prepare for a family gathering, Sara and Ryan made soup.
Sara made 2 quarts. Ryan made 6 quarts.

You can compare amounts using multiplication and division.

Let r equal the number of quarts Ryan made.
Let s equal the number of quarts Sara made.

Ryan made 3 times as many quarts as Sara.

$$r = 3 \cdot s$$

Ryan (r) | 2 | 2 | 2 | 6

Sarah (s) | 2

Sara made one third as many quarts as Ryan.

$$s = \frac{1}{3} \cdot r \text{ or } s = r \div 3$$

Solve.

Natasha made 12 quarts of soup. Manuel made 3 quarts.

Show your work on your paper or in your journal.

9. Draw **comparison bars** to show the amount of soup each person made.

10. _____ made 4 times as many quarts as _____.

11. _____ made $\frac{1}{4}$ as many quarts as _____.

12. Write two multiplication equations that compare the amounts.

$n = $ _____ $m = $ _____

13. Write a division equation that compares the amounts.

Basic Multiplication Concepts

▶ Solve Comparison Problems

Solve.

Show your work on your paper or in your journal.

In the gym, 8 girls are standing in one line and 4 boys are standing in another line.

14. Draw comparison bars to compare the number of people in each line.

15. Write two multiplication equations that compare the number of girls (*g*) to the number of boys (*b*).

    g = _____   *b* = _____

16. Write a division equation that compares the number of boys (*b*) to the number of girls (*g*).

17. A collection of coins contains 20 pennies and 4 nickels.

    Write two multiplication equations and a division equation that compare the number of pennies (*p*) and the number of nickels (*n*).

    _____   _____   _____

18. A fifth-grade class is made up of 12 boys and 24 girls. How many times as many girls as boys are in the class?

19. Fred has 24 football cards. Scott has $\frac{1}{6}$ as many football cards as Fred. How many football cards does Scott have?

▶ Compare Data in Graphs and Tables

20. How many times as many fish did Bill catch as Amy?

Fish Caught at the Lake

21. How many times as many fish did Amy catch as Bill?

22. What is $\frac{1}{3} \cdot 15$? What is $15 \div 3$? What is $\frac{15}{3}$?

Write two statements for each pair of players. Use the word *times.*

23. Compare Gina's points and Brent's points.

**Points at the
Basketball Game**

Player	Points
Gina	32
Brent	8
Jacob	4

24. Compare Brent's points and Jacob's points.

25. Compare Jacob's points and Gina's points.

26. Which are the shortest and longest snakes?
How do you know?

**Length of Snakes
at the Zoo**

Snake	Inches
Speedy	n
Lola	$\frac{1}{5} \cdot n$
Pretzel	$5 \cdot n$

27. If Speedy is 25 inches long, how long is Lola?

28. If Pretzel is 50 inches long, how long is Speedy?
How long is Lola?

▶ Visualize the Separate Steps

Silver City is 24 miles away. Gus has driven $\frac{1}{4}$ of the distance. Emma has driven $\frac{3}{4}$ of the distance.

1. How many miles has Gus driven?

2. How many miles has Emma driven?

3. How many times as far as Gus has Emma driven?

4. If $\frac{1}{5}$ of a distance is 3 km, how far is $\frac{4}{5}$?

5. If $\frac{1}{8}$ of a container weighs 2 pounds, how many pounds is $\frac{3}{8}$ of the container?

6. If $\frac{1}{7}$ of a book is 4 pages, how many pages is $\frac{2}{7}$ of the book?

Shady Grove is 40 miles away. Middletown is $\frac{1}{5}$ of the way there and Parkview is $\frac{2}{5}$ of the way.

7. How many miles away is Middletown?

8. How many miles away is Parkview?

9. Ocean City is 42 miles from home. We have gone 35 miles. What fraction of the distance have we gone?

10. Eagle Rock is 72 miles away. When we had gone $\frac{2}{9}$ of the distance, we stopped for gas. How many miles had we traveled?

11. Perilous Peak is 80 miles away. We are $\frac{3}{10}$ of the way there. How many more miles do we have to go?

12. Windy Bay is 48 miles away. Make up your own fraction word problem with multiplication. Be sure to include a non-unit fraction.

VOCABULARY
factor
product

▶ Practice Multiplication with Fractions

Solve the problem pairs.

13. $\frac{1}{3}$ of 18 = ▨

 $\frac{2}{3}$ of 18 = ▨

14. $\frac{1}{4} \cdot 32$ = ▨

 $\frac{3}{4} \cdot 32$ = ▨

15. $\frac{1}{9} \cdot 27$ = ▨

 $\frac{4}{9} \cdot 27$ = ▨

16. $\frac{1}{6} \cdot 42$ = ▨

 $\frac{5}{6} \cdot 42$ = ▨

Parts of a Multiplication Problem
$\frac{3}{5} \cdot 10 = 6$
factor   factor   product

17. Which expression does *not* have the same value as the others?

 $\frac{2}{3} \cdot 21$ $\frac{2}{3}$ of 21 $\left(\frac{1}{3} \text{ of } 21\right) + \left(\frac{1}{3} \text{ of } 21\right)$

 $\frac{2}{3} + 21$ $\frac{21}{3} + \frac{21}{3}$ $\left(\frac{1}{3} \text{ of } 21\right) \cdot 2$

Use the table to answer each question.

18. Which building is the tallest? Which is the shortest? How do you know?

Building	Number of Stories
Bank	n
Bus station	$\frac{1}{6} \cdot n$
Sport shop	$\frac{5}{6} \cdot n$
Hotel	$6 \cdot n$

Suppose the bus station is 2 stories tall.

19. How many stories does the sport shop have?

20. How many stories does the bank have?

Suppose the bank is 5 stories tall.

21. How many stories tall is the hotel?

Suppose the hotel is 36 stories tall.

22. How many stories does the bank have?

23. How many stories does the bus station have?

24. How many stories does the sport shop have?

Multiplication with Non-Unit Fractions

Use Activity Workbook page 30.

▶ Model the Product $\frac{1}{d} \cdot w$

Farmer Diaz has 3 acres of land. He plows $\frac{1}{5}$ of this land. The number of acres he plows is

$\frac{1}{5}$ of 3 or $\frac{1}{5} \cdot 3$

The diagram at the right shows Farmer Diaz's land divided vertically into 3 acres. The dashed horizontal segments divide the land into five parts. The shaded strip is the $\frac{1}{5}$ of the land Farmer Diaz plowed.

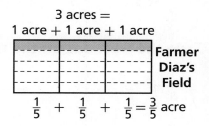

3 acres = 1 acre + 1 acre + 1 acre

Farmer Diaz's Field

$\frac{1}{5} + \frac{1}{5} + \frac{1}{5} = \frac{3}{5}$ acre

The drawing shows that taking $\frac{1}{5}$ of the 3 acres is the same as taking $\frac{1}{5}$ of each acre and combining them. We can show this mathematically.

$$\frac{1}{5} \cdot 3 = \frac{1}{5}(1 + 1 + 1)$$
$$= \left(\frac{1}{5} \cdot 1\right) + \left(\frac{1}{5} \cdot 1\right) + \left(\frac{1}{5} \cdot 1\right)$$
$$= \frac{1}{5} + \frac{1}{5} + \frac{1}{5}$$
$$= \frac{3}{5}$$

So $\frac{1}{5}$ of the 3 acres is $\frac{3}{5}$ acre.

1. Farmer Smith has 4 acres of land. She plows $\frac{1}{3}$ of her land. Divide and shade the drawing at the right to show the part of the land she plows.

4 acres = 1 acre + 1 acre + 1 acre + 1 acre

2. Express $\frac{1}{3} \cdot 4$ as a sum of unit fractions.

$\frac{1}{3} \cdot 4 = $ ▨

3. What area does Farmer Smith plow?

4. Farmer Hanson plows $\frac{1}{7}$ of his 2 acres of land. What area does he plow?

5. Olga walks 9 blocks to school. Her friend Louis walks only $\frac{1}{5}$ of that distance. How many blocks does Louis walk to school?

Use Activity
Workbook page 31.

▶ Multiply by a Non-Unit Fraction

6. Which expression does *not* have the same value as the others?

$\frac{1}{4}$ of 3 $\frac{1}{4} \cdot 3$ $4 \cdot \frac{1}{3}$ $\frac{1}{4} + \frac{1}{4} + \frac{1}{4}$ $3 \cdot \frac{1}{4}$

Circle the fractions on the number lines to help you multiply.

7. a. $\frac{1}{7} \cdot 2 = $ ▢

b. $\frac{3}{7} \cdot 2 = $ ▢

8. a. $\frac{1}{5} \cdot 3 = $ ▢

b. $\frac{4}{5} \cdot 3 = $ ▢

9. a. $\frac{1}{6} \cdot 4 = $ ▢

b. $\frac{5}{6} \cdot 4 = $ ▢

10. a. $\frac{1}{3} \cdot 8 = $ ▢

b. $\frac{2}{3} \cdot 8 = $ ▢

Multiplication with Fractional Solutions

Use Activity
Workbook page 32.

▶ Use Bar Models to Multiply Fractions

Miguel explains how to use fraction bars to find $\frac{2}{3} \cdot \frac{4}{5}$:

First, I circle 4 fifths on the fifths fraction bar.

To find $\frac{2}{3}$ of $\frac{4}{5}$, I can circle $\frac{2}{3}$ of each fifth. But, first I have to split each fifth into three parts. After I do this, the bar is divided into fifteenths.

Now, it is easy to circle 2 thirds of each of the 4 fifths.

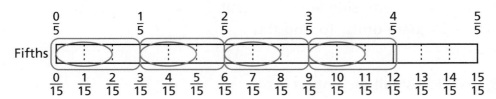

Each group I circled has 2 fifteenths, so I circled 4 groups of 2 fifteenths. That's 8 fifteenths in all. So, $\frac{2}{3} \cdot \frac{4}{5} = \frac{8}{15}$.

1. Use the sixths bar below to model $\frac{3}{4} \cdot \frac{5}{6}$.

$\frac{3}{4} \cdot \frac{5}{6} = \blacksquare$

Sixths

2. Use the sevenths bar below to model $\frac{2}{3} \cdot \frac{4}{7}$.

$\frac{2}{3} \cdot \frac{4}{7} = \blacksquare$

Sevenths

Use Activity
Workbook page 33.

▶ Use Area Models to Multiply Fractions

Jessie knows that the area of a rectangle is its length times its width. She explains how to use this idea to model $\frac{2}{3} \cdot \frac{4}{5}$:

I need to draw a rectangle with side lengths $\frac{2}{3}$ unit and $\frac{4}{5}$ unit.

I start with a unit square and divide it vertically into fifths. Then I shade $\frac{4}{5}$.

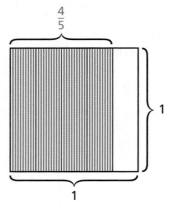

Next, I divide the square horizontally into thirds, and shade $\frac{2}{3}$.

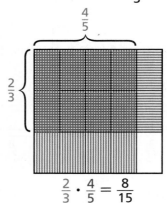

$$\frac{2}{3} \cdot \frac{4}{5} = \frac{8}{15}$$

The overlapping part is a rectangle with side lengths $\frac{2}{3}$ unit and $\frac{4}{5}$ unit. So, its area is $\frac{2}{3} \cdot \frac{4}{5}$ square units. To find this area, I noticed the following:

▶ There are 3 · 5, or 15, identical small rectangles inside the unit square. Each one is $\frac{1}{15}$ square unit, so it represents the unit fraction $\frac{1}{15}$.

▶ There are 2 · 4, or 8, of these unit-fraction rectangles inside the $\frac{2}{3}$ by $\frac{4}{5}$ rectangle.

So the area of the overlapping region is $8 \cdot \frac{1}{15}$, or $\frac{8}{15}$ square units. This means $\frac{2}{3} \cdot \frac{4}{5} = \frac{8}{15}$.

Divide and shade the unit square to make an area model for the multiplication. Then find the product.

3. $\frac{1}{2} \cdot \frac{3}{8} = $ �In

4. $\frac{3}{4} \cdot \frac{2}{3} = $ ▇

5. $\frac{5}{6} \cdot \frac{1}{3} = $ ▇

Multiply a Fraction by a Fraction

► Practice Multiplying Fractions

Find the product. You do not need to simplify your answer.

6. $\frac{1}{7} \cdot 6 =$ ▧

7. $5 \cdot \frac{1}{4} =$ ▧

8. $\frac{2}{3} \cdot 9 =$ ▧

9. $4 \cdot \frac{3}{8} =$ ▧

10. $\frac{1}{9} \cdot \frac{1}{2} =$ ▧

11. $\frac{1}{3} \cdot \frac{1}{4} =$ ▧

12. $\frac{2}{5} \cdot \frac{1}{3} =$ ▧

13. $\frac{5}{6} \cdot \frac{3}{4} =$ ▧

14. $\frac{3}{7} \cdot \frac{1}{3} =$ ▧

15. $\frac{7}{10} \cdot \frac{7}{10} =$ ▧

16. $\frac{3}{4} \cdot \frac{6}{11} =$ ▧

17. $\frac{7}{8} \cdot \frac{8}{9} =$ ▧

18. $\frac{4}{5} \cdot \frac{4}{5} =$ ▧

19. $\frac{2}{7} \cdot \frac{4}{9} =$ ▧

20. $\frac{4}{7} \cdot \frac{2}{9} =$ ▧

21. $\frac{3}{4} \cdot 20 =$ ▧

22. $\frac{1}{10} \cdot \frac{1}{10} =$ ▧

23. $6 \cdot \frac{2}{3} =$ ▧

24. $\frac{7}{8} \cdot \frac{1}{3} =$ ▧

25. $\frac{7}{10} \cdot \frac{2}{7} =$ ▧

26. $\frac{2}{5} \cdot 12 =$ ▧

27. $\frac{1}{4} \cdot \frac{1}{2} =$ ▧

28. $\frac{1}{5} \cdot 5 =$ ▧

29. $\frac{6}{7} \cdot \frac{7}{8} =$ ▧

▶ Fraction Word Problems

Represent the problem with an equation. Then solve.

Show your work on your paper or in your journal.

30. Of the 304 people who attended the school play, $\frac{5}{8}$ were students. How many of the people who attended were students?

31. One lap around the track is $\frac{1}{4}$ mile. Abby ran around the track 13 times. How far did she run?

32. Cam is filling his bathtub. The tub holds 32 gallons of water. It is now $\frac{4}{7}$ full. How many gallons of water are in the tub?

33. One third of the campers at a summer camp signed up for an arts-and-crafts class. Of these campers, one fifth signed up for woodworking. What fraction of the campers signed up for woodworking?

34. Two thirds of the students in the orchestra play string instruments. Half of the students who play string instruments play violins. What fraction of all the students in the orchestra play violins?

35. Ms. Hernandez knitted a scarf for her grandson. The scarf is $\frac{5}{6}$ yard long and $\frac{2}{9}$ yard wide. What is the area of the scarf?

Multiply a Fraction by a Fraction

▶ Simplify and Multiply Fractions

Multiply. Simplify first if you can.

1. $\frac{2}{3} \cdot 30 =$ ▨

2. $\frac{2}{5} \cdot 35 =$ ▨

3. $\frac{5}{6} \cdot 4 =$ ▨

4. $\frac{7}{16} \cdot 8 =$ ▨

5. $\frac{7}{20} \cdot \frac{5}{14} =$ ▨

6. $\frac{2}{16} \cdot \frac{4}{21} =$ ▨

7. $\frac{9}{10} \cdot \frac{7}{10} =$ ▨

8. $\frac{7}{15} \cdot \frac{10}{21} =$ ▨

9. $\frac{5}{24} \cdot \frac{6}{25} =$ ▨

10. $\frac{5}{8} \cdot \frac{32}{45} =$ ▨

11. $\frac{8}{49} \cdot \frac{7}{10} =$ ▨

12. $\frac{7}{25} \cdot \frac{3}{4} =$ ▨

13. Which fraction is not equivalent to the others?

$\frac{3}{9}$ $\qquad$ $\frac{1}{3}$ $\qquad$ $\frac{8}{24}$ $\qquad$ $\frac{10}{30}$ $\qquad$ $\frac{6}{18}$ $\qquad$ $\frac{9}{36}$ $\qquad$ $\frac{20}{60}$

▶ Solve Word Problems

Write an equation. Then solve.

Show your work on your paper or in your journal.

14. In the Fireside Ski Shop, $\frac{11}{28}$ of the ski caps have tassels. Of the caps with tassels, $\frac{7}{11}$ are blue. What fraction of the caps in the shop are blue with tassels?

15. In the shop, $\frac{27}{32}$ of the jackets have zippers. Of the jackets with zippers, $\frac{8}{9}$ have hoods. What fraction of the jackets in the shop have both zippers and hoods?

16. Five of the 16 workers in the shop know how to ski. $\frac{1}{5}$ of those who can ski know how to snowboard. What fraction of the workers can ski and snowboard?

▶ What's the Error?

Dear Math Students,

I multiplied $\frac{7}{12} \cdot \frac{3}{4}$, but I think my answer is wrong. When you take a fraction of a fraction, you should get a smaller fraction. But my answer is larger. What mistake did I make? How do I correct it?

$$\frac{7}{\cancel{12}_3} \cdot \frac{3}{\cancel{4}_1} = \frac{21}{3} = 7$$

Your friend,
Puzzled Penguin

17. Write a response to Puzzled Penguin.

▶ Write Word Problems

Write a word problem that can be represented by the multiplication. Give the solution to your problem.

18. $\frac{3}{4} \cdot 8 = x$

19. $\frac{8}{15} \cdot \frac{5}{12} = x$

▶ Area Model for Mixed-Number Multiplication

A farmer has a rectangular field $1\frac{2}{3}$ miles long and $\frac{3}{4}$ mile wide. What is the area of the field?

Melinda knows the area is $1\frac{2}{3} \cdot \frac{3}{4}$. She explains how she makes an area model to find this product:

I need to make a rectangle with side lengths $1\frac{2}{3}$ units and $\frac{3}{4}$ unit. I start with 2 unit squares because one side of my rectangle will have a length greater than 1 unit.

I shade $\frac{3}{4}$ vertically in red. Horizontally, I shade 1 square and $\frac{2}{3}$ of another in blue. The overlap has an area of $1\frac{2}{3} \cdot \frac{3}{4}$, but I can't tell what this area is.

I divide the top square horizontally into thirds too. So, $\frac{5}{3}$ is shaded horizontally. Now, I can see that each unit square is divided into twelfths.

There are 15 twelfths in the overlap, so $1\frac{2}{3} \cdot \frac{3}{4} = \frac{15}{12}$, which is $1\frac{1}{4}$. The area of the field is $1\frac{1}{4}$ miles.

When I rewrite the factor $1\frac{2}{3}$ as a fraction, I can see that the product is the product of the numerators over the product of the denominators.

$$1\frac{2}{3} \cdot \frac{3}{4} = \frac{5}{3} \cdot \frac{3}{4} = \frac{15}{12} = \frac{5}{4} = 1\frac{1}{4}$$

Discuss this model for $1\frac{2}{5} \cdot 1\frac{1}{2}$ with your partner. Then answer the questions.

1. What unit fraction does each of the smallest rectangles represent?

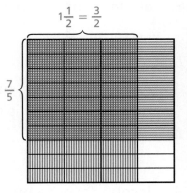

$1\frac{1}{2} = \frac{3}{2}$

$1\frac{2}{5} = \frac{7}{5}$

2. How many unit-fraction rectangles are in the overlap?

3. Express the product of $1\frac{2}{5} \cdot 1\frac{1}{2}$ as a fraction and as a mixed number.

4. Rewrite $1\frac{2}{5} \cdot 1\frac{1}{2}$ as a product of fractions. Is the product equal to the product of the numerators over the product of the denominators?

▶ Practice Multiplying Mixed Numbers

Find each product by first rewriting each mixed number as a fraction.

5. $\frac{5}{6} \cdot 1\frac{1}{3} = $ ▨

6. $3\frac{2}{3} \cdot 7 = $ ▨

7. $1\frac{3}{4} \cdot 2\frac{1}{4} = $ ▨

8. $4\frac{1}{2} \cdot \frac{4}{5} = $ ▨

9. $\frac{7}{8} \cdot 1\frac{2}{5} = $ ▨

10. $5 \cdot 1\frac{7}{10} = $ ▨

11. $1\frac{2}{3} \cdot 1\frac{2}{3} = $ ▨

12. $\frac{1}{12} \cdot 2\frac{2}{9} = $ ▨

▶ Solve Word Problems

Represent the problem with an equation. Then solve. Draw a diagram if you need to.

Show your work on your paper or in your journal.

13. Sara built a pen for her pet rabbits. The pen measures $2\frac{5}{6}$ yards by $1\frac{1}{2}$ yards. What is the area of the pen?

14. At Southtown High School, the number of students in band is $1\frac{3}{4}$ times the number in orchestra. If 56 students are in orchestra, how many are in band?

15. A bucket holds $2\frac{3}{4}$ gallons of water. The bucket is $\frac{5}{8}$ full. How much water is in the bucket?

16. Jacob's favorite movie is $1\frac{5}{6}$ hours long. He says he has watched the movie $5\frac{1}{2}$ times. If that is true, how many hours has Jacob spent watching the movie?

Use Activity
Workbook page 34.

▶ Compare Multiplication and Addition

These fraction bars show how we add and multiply fractions.

Add $\frac{2}{5} + \frac{3}{5} = \frac{5}{5}$

Take $\frac{2}{5}$ of the whole

Multiply $\frac{3}{5} \cdot \frac{2}{5} = \frac{6}{25}$

Then take $\frac{3}{5}$ of each fifth.

1. Which problem above has the greater answer?

2. Circle the problem that will have the greater answer. Then solve.

    $\frac{2}{7} + \frac{3}{7} = \blacksquare$ $\frac{3}{7} \cdot \frac{2}{7} = \blacksquare$

3. The fractions in the problems at the right have different denominators. problem Circle the that will have the greater answer. Then solve.

    $\frac{1}{6} + \frac{3}{4} = \blacksquare$ $\frac{3}{4} \cdot \frac{1}{6} = \blacksquare$

▶ Compare Fraction and Whole-Number Operations

Tell whether the answer will be less than or greater than the red number.

4. $a + b$ 5. $a - b$ 6. $b \cdot a$

7. $\frac{a}{b} + \frac{c}{d}$ 8. $\frac{a}{b} - \frac{c}{d}$ 9. $\frac{c}{d} \cdot \frac{a}{b}$

10. How is multiplying fractions different from multiplying whole numbers?

Keep in Mind

a and b are whole numbers greater than 1.

All of the fractions are less than 1.

▶ Comparison Problems with Mixed Operations

Amber, a very fit snail, moved $\frac{7}{9}$ yard in an hour. She challenged the other snails to try to do better.

Write how far each snail went.

11. Willy moved $\frac{4}{5}$ as far as Amber.

12. Dusty went $\frac{1}{3}$ yard less than Amber.

13. Pearl went twice as far as Amber.

14. Casey moved $\frac{4}{9}$ yard more than Amber.

15. Minnie moved half as far as Amber.

16. Make up your own question about another snail, Shelly. Ask a classmate to solve it.

▶ Properties and Fractions

Commutative Property of Multiplication

$$\frac{a}{b} \cdot \frac{c}{d} = \frac{c}{d} \cdot \frac{a}{b}$$

Look at the proof of the **Commutative Property** below.

$$\frac{a}{b} \cdot \frac{c}{d} \quad = \quad \underset{\text{Step 1}}{\frac{a \cdot c}{b \cdot d}} \quad = \quad \underset{\text{Step 2}}{\frac{c \cdot a}{d \cdot b}} \quad = \quad \underset{\text{Step 3}}{\frac{c}{d} \cdot \frac{a}{b}}$$

17. Explain why each step is true.

    Step 1

    Step 2

    Step 3

► Properties and Fractions (continued)

Associative Property of Multiplication

$$\frac{a}{b} \cdot \left(\frac{c}{d} \cdot \frac{e}{f}\right) = \left(\frac{a}{b} \cdot \frac{c}{d}\right) \cdot \frac{e}{f}$$

Look at the proof of the **Associative Property** below.

$$\frac{a}{b} \cdot \left(\frac{c}{d} \cdot \frac{e}{f}\right) = \frac{a}{b} \cdot \frac{c \cdot e}{d \cdot f} = \frac{a \cdot (c \cdot e)}{b \cdot (d \cdot f)} = \frac{(a \cdot c) \cdot e}{(b \cdot d) \cdot f} = \frac{a \cdot c}{b \cdot d} \cdot \frac{e}{f} = \left(\frac{a}{b} \cdot \frac{c}{d}\right) \cdot \frac{e}{f}$$

Step 1   Step 2   Step 3   Step 4   Step 5

18. Explain why each step is true.

Step 1

Step 2

Step 3

Step 4

Step 5

Distributive Property

$$\frac{a}{b} \cdot \left(\frac{c}{d} + \frac{e}{f}\right) = \frac{a}{b} \cdot \frac{c}{d} + \frac{a}{b} \cdot \frac{e}{f}$$

For example, the **Distributive Property** tells us that

$$\frac{1}{2} \cdot \left(\frac{2}{3} + \frac{1}{4}\right) = \frac{1}{2} \cdot \frac{2}{3} + \frac{1}{2} \cdot \frac{1}{4}$$

19. Find the value of $\frac{1}{2} \cdot \left(\frac{2}{3} + \frac{1}{4}\right)$ by adding inside the parentheses first and then multiplying.

20. Find the value of $\frac{1}{2} \cdot \frac{2}{3} + \frac{1}{2} \cdot \frac{1}{4}$ by multiplying and then adding.

21. How do your answers to Exercises 19 and 20 compare?

▶ Mixed Practice

Find the value of the expression.

22. $\frac{4}{5} \cdot \frac{3}{7}$

23. $\frac{4}{5} - \frac{3}{7}$

24. $6 \cdot 1\frac{1}{3}$

25. $6 + 1\frac{1}{3}$

26. $1\frac{1}{2} + \frac{2}{3}$

27. $1\frac{1}{2} \cdot \frac{2}{3}$

28. $\frac{5}{8} \cdot \frac{8}{5}$

29. $\frac{5}{8} + \frac{8}{5}$

Show your work on your paper or in your journal.

Write an equation. Then solve.

30. Daniel puts some wheat flour into an empty bowl. Then he adds $\frac{2}{3}$ cup rye flour to make a total of $2\frac{5}{12}$ cups of flour. How much wheat flour is in the bowl?

31. Mañuela has a bag containing $5\frac{1}{3}$ cups of sugar. She uses $\frac{1}{8}$ of the sugar in a recipe. How much sugar does she use?

32. Ashanti has a bag that contains $4\frac{1}{4}$ cups of rice. She uses $\frac{2}{3}$ cup. How much rice is left in the bag?

33. Seth's route to school is $1\frac{3}{10}$ miles long. He has walked $\frac{4}{5}$ mile so far. How much farther does he have to go?

34. Mara's walk to school is $1\frac{2}{5}$ miles. She is $\frac{5}{8}$ of the way there. How far has she walked so far?

Relate Fraction Operations

Use Activity Workbook page 35.

▶ Add, Subtract, Compare, and Multiply

The fraction box to the right shows the same two fractions compared, added, subtracted, and multiplied.

	$\frac{1}{3}$ and $\frac{1}{6}$
>	$\frac{1}{3} > \frac{1}{6}$ or $\frac{2}{6} > \frac{1}{6}$
+	$\frac{1}{3} + \frac{1}{6} = \frac{2}{6} + \frac{1}{6} = \frac{3}{6} = \frac{1}{2}$
−	$\frac{1}{3} - \frac{1}{6} = \frac{2}{6} - \frac{1}{6} = \frac{1}{6}$
·	$\frac{1}{3} \cdot \frac{1}{6} = \frac{1}{18}$

Complete the fraction box.

1.

	$\frac{2}{5}$ and $\frac{7}{10}$
>	
+	
−	
·	

2.

	$\frac{3}{5}$ and $\frac{4}{7}$
>	
+	
−	
·	

▶ What's the Error?

Dear Math Students,

One of my friends said that he would give $\frac{1}{2}$ of his sandwich to me and $\frac{1}{2}$ of his sandwich to my sister. My sister said, "But then you won't have any left for yourself." This doesn't make sense to me. I know that $\frac{1}{2} + \frac{1}{2} = \frac{2}{4}$. My friend should have plenty left for himself. Did I do something wrong? What do you think?

Puzzled Penguin

3. Write a response to Puzzled Penguin.

▶ Word Problems with Mixed Operations

Solve.

Show your work on your paper or in your journal.

4. Yesterday Mr. Swenson made $2\frac{3}{4}$ quarts of strawberry jam and $1\frac{1}{8}$ quarts of raspberry jam. How much more strawberry jam did he make than raspberry?

5. Today Mr. Swenson is making $\frac{2}{5}$ quart of grape jelly. He will give $\frac{1}{2}$ of this amount to his neighbor. How much jelly will the neighbor get?

6. Mr. Swenson is also making $2\frac{1}{6}$ quarts of cherry jelly and $3\frac{1}{12}$ quarts of orange jelly. He will mix the two kinds together. How much of this mixed jelly will he have?

7. Yesterday Mr. Swenson made $\frac{7}{10}$ quart of blueberry jam. His family ate $\frac{1}{10}$ of it. How much of the blueberry jam is left?

8. Suppose Mr. Swenson has jars that hold $\frac{5}{6}$ quart, jars that hold $\frac{3}{4}$ quart, and jars that hold $\frac{2}{3}$ quart. Which size holds the most? Which size holds the least? How do you know?

9. Mr. Swenson made $6\frac{2}{3}$ quarts of jam last weekend. This weekend he plans to make $1\frac{1}{2}$ times this much. How much jam will he make this weekend?

Solve Real World Problems

Use Activity
Workbook page 36.

▶ Predict and Multiply

Predict whether the product will be greater than, less than, or equal to the second factor. Then compute the product.

1. $\frac{2}{5} \cdot \frac{3}{4} = x$

Predict: x ◯ $\frac{3}{4}$

Compute: $x =$ ▨

2. $\frac{6}{6} \cdot \frac{3}{4} = x$

Predict: x ◯ $\frac{3}{4}$

Compute: $x =$ ▨

3. $1\frac{3}{7} \cdot \frac{3}{4} = x$

Predict: x ◯ $\frac{3}{4}$

Compute: $x =$ ▨

4. $\frac{3}{3} \cdot 2\frac{1}{2} = x$

Predict: x ◯ $2\frac{1}{2}$

Compute: $x =$ ▨

5. $2\frac{2}{3} \cdot 2\frac{1}{2} = x$

Predict: x ◯ $2\frac{1}{2}$

Compute: $x =$ ▨

6. $\frac{7}{8} \cdot 2\frac{1}{2} = x$

Predict: x ◯ $2\frac{1}{2}$

Compute: $x =$ ▨

7. $1\frac{1}{10} \cdot 5 = x$

Predict: x ◯ 5

Compute: $x =$ ▨

8. $\frac{9}{10} \cdot 5 = x$

Predict: x ◯ 5

Compute: $x =$ ▨

9. $\frac{10}{10} \cdot 5 = x$

Predict: x ◯ 5

Compute: $x =$ ▨

▶ Generalize

Complete the statement with *greater than*, *less than*, or *equal to*.

10. Multiplying any number, *n*, by a factor less than 1 gives a product _____ ▨ _____ *n*.

11. Multiplying any number, *n*, by a factor equal to 1 gives a product _____ ▨ _____ *n*.

12. Multiplying any number, *n*, by a factor greater than 1 gives a product _____ ▨ _____ *n*.

Multiplying a fraction by a fraction equal to 1 gives an equivalent fraction. It is the same as multiplying both the numerator and denominator by the same number.

$$\frac{4}{7} = \frac{4}{7} \cdot \frac{3}{3} = \frac{12}{21} \qquad \frac{4}{7} = \frac{4 \cdot 3}{7 \cdot 3} = \frac{12}{21}$$

Multiply the fraction by a factor equal to 1 to create an equivalent fraction.

13. $\frac{4}{5}$

14. $\frac{3}{11}$

15. $\frac{5}{8}$

► **Predict and Solve**

Solve.

Show your work on your paper or in your journal.

16. A box of granola weighs 18 ounces. A box of corn flakes weighs $\frac{7}{9}$ as much as the granola.

    Do the corn flakes weigh more or less than 18 ounces?

    How much do the corn flakes weigh?

17. A rectangle has length $3\frac{1}{4}$ feet and width $1\frac{1}{3}$ feet.

    Is the area of the rectangle greater or less than $3\frac{1}{4}$ square feet?

    What is the area of the rectangle?

18. The number of students on the football team is $1\frac{3}{4}$ times the number on the basketball team. There are 16 students on the basketball team.

    Are there more or fewer than 16 students on the football team?

    How many students are on the football team?

19. It's $9\frac{4}{5}$ miles from Justin's house to the art museum. The distance to the history museum is $\frac{9}{10}$ this far.

    Is the history museum more or less than $9\frac{4}{5}$ miles from Justin's house?

    How far from Justin's house is the history museum?

Make Generalizations

Use Activity Workbook page 37.

▶ Explore Fractional Shares

There are 4 people in the Walton family, but there are only 3 waffles. How can the Waltons share the waffles equally?

Divide each waffle into 4 pieces.

Each person's share of one waffle is $\frac{1}{4}$. Since there are 3 waffles, each person gets 3 of the $\frac{1}{4}$s, or $\frac{3}{4}$ of a whole waffle.

$$3 \div 4 = 3 \cdot \frac{1}{4} = \frac{3}{4}$$

1. Suppose there are 5 people and 4 waffles.

   What is each person's share of 1 waffle?

   What is each person's share of 4 waffles?

   Complete the equation: $4 \div 5 = $ _____ $\cdot$ _____ = _____

2. Suppose there are 10 people and 7 waffles.

   What is each person's share of 1 waffle?

   What is each person's share of 7 waffles?

   Complete the equation: $7 \div 10 = $ _____ $\cdot$ _____ = _____

Complete.

3. $5 \div 6 = $ _____ $\cdot$ _____ = _____

4. $4 \div 9 = $ _____ $\cdot$ _____ = _____

Give your answer in the form of an equation.

5. How can you divide 7 waffles equally among 8 people?

6. How can you divide 39 waffles equally among 5 serving plates?

7. Discuss why this equation is true for any whole numbers n and d, except $d = 0$.

$$n \div d = n \cdot \frac{1}{d} = \frac{n}{d}$$

n unit fractions $\frac{1}{d}$

▶ Divide by a Unit Fraction

8. How many $\frac{1}{8}$s are there in 1? Write a division equation to show this.

one whole

9. How many $\frac{1}{8}$s are there in 3? Write a division equation to show this.

10. Why can you also use the multiplication equation $3 \cdot 8 = 24$ to show how many $\frac{1}{8}$s are in 3?

11. How many $\frac{1}{4}$s are there in 5? Write a division and a multiplication equation to show this.

12. Complete the equation. w and d are whole numbers and d is not 0. $w \div \frac{1}{d} = \blacksquare$

Show your work on your paper or in your journal.

Write a division equation. Then solve.

13. Olivia made 9 sandwiches and cut each one into fourths. How many fourths does she have?

14. The 10 members of a hiking club will walk 9 miles. Each person will carry the food pack for an equal distance. How far will each hiker carry the food pack?

15. Damon has a 6-pound bag of cat food. He feeds his cat $\frac{1}{8}$ pound every day. How many days will the bag last?

16. Jodie and 7 friends share 12 oranges equally. How many oranges does each person get? Give your answer as a mixed number.

▶ Unit Fractions in Action

Karen's 5 grandchildren came to visit for 3 days. Karen found a long roll of drawing paper. She said, "I'll cut this paper into 3 equal parts, and we'll use one part on each day." Then she cut the first part into 5 equal parts so each grandchild could make a drawing. She asked her grandchildren, "What part of the whole roll of paper do each of you have? What math problem is this? Make a drawing so Sammy will understand."

Tommy, the oldest, said, "Today we are using $\frac{1}{3}$ of the whole roll because we have 3 equal parts."

$$\frac{1}{3}$$

Lucy said, "Then we cut that $\frac{1}{3}$ into 5 equal parts. So we found $\frac{1}{3} \div 5$, a unit fraction divided by the whole number 5."

$$\frac{1}{3} \div 5$$

Asha said, "But we have to divide each of the other two thirds into 5 equal parts to find out how many equal parts we have in all. That's like multiplying by $\frac{1}{5}$!"

$$\frac{1}{3} \cdot \frac{1}{5}$$

Phoebe said, "Oh look, we have 15 equal parts in all. So today we are each using $\frac{1}{15}$ of the whole roll."

$$\frac{1}{3} \cdot \frac{1}{5} = \frac{1}{15}$$

Sammy, the youngest grandchild said, "So dividing by 5 is the same as multiplying by $\frac{1}{5}$ because that also means finding one of five equal parts."

$$\frac{1}{3} \div 5 = \frac{1}{3} \cdot \frac{1}{5} = \frac{1}{15}$$

The children said, "So dividing by a whole number w is the same as multiplying by $\frac{1}{w}$."

$$\frac{1}{d} \div w = \frac{1}{d} \cdot \frac{1}{w} = \frac{1}{d \cdot w}$$

Solve.

17. $\frac{1}{2} \div 3 = \frac{1}{2} \cdot \blacksquare = \blacksquare$

18. $\frac{1}{5} \div 2 = \frac{1}{5} \cdot \blacksquare = \blacksquare$

19. $\frac{1}{3} \div 4 = \frac{1}{3} \cdot \blacksquare = \blacksquare$

20. $\frac{1}{6} \div 4 = \frac{1}{6} \cdot \blacksquare = \blacksquare$

Use Activity
Workbook page 38.

▶ Practice Division

$$n \div d = n \cdot \frac{1}{d} = \frac{n}{d} \qquad w \div \frac{1}{d} = w \cdot d \qquad \frac{1}{d} \div w = \frac{1}{d} \cdot \frac{1}{w} = \frac{1}{d \cdot w}$$

21. Describe patterns you see in the equations above.

22. Why is dividing by a whole number the same as multiplying by a unit fraction with that number as its denominator?

23. Why does dividing w by a unit fraction $\frac{1}{d}$ make $w \cdot d$, a number greater than w?

24. $3 \div 10 = $ ▧ $\cdot$ ▧ $= $ ▧
25. $5 \div 8 = $ ▧ $\cdot$ ▧ $= $ ▧

26. $4 \div \frac{1}{3} = $ ▧ $\cdot$ ▧ $= $ ▧
27. $7 \div \frac{1}{2} = $ ▧ $\cdot$ ▧ $= $ ▧

28. $\frac{1}{2} \div 5 = $ ▧ $\cdot$ ▧ $= $ ▧
29. $\frac{1}{3} \div 4 = $ ▧ $\cdot$ ▧ $= $ ▧

30. For the two problems below, which answer will be greater? Explain.

$$\frac{1}{3} \div 5 \qquad\qquad 5 \div \frac{1}{3}$$

When Dividing Is Also Multiplying

Use Activity
Workbook page 39.

► Division Situations and Diagrams

1. Consider the division problem $2 \div 5$.

   Describe a situation this division could represent.

   Draw a diagram to represent the division. Then find the solution.

2. Consider the division problem $4 \div \frac{1}{3}$.

   Describe a situation this division could represent.

   Draw a diagram to represent the division. Then find the solution.

3. Consider the division problem $\frac{1}{4} \div 2$.

   Describe a situation this division could represent.

   Draw a diagram to represent the division. Then find the solution.

Show your work on your paper or in your journal.

▶ Division Word Problems

Write an equation. Then solve.

4. One lap around the track is $\frac{1}{4}$ mile. José wants to run 5 miles. How many times must he run around the track?

5. There is $\frac{1}{6}$ of an extra large pizza left over in the fridge. If three friends share the pizza equally, what fraction of a whole pizza will each friend get?

6. Oscar's aunt lives 50 miles away. This is 6 times as far as Oscar's grandfather lives. How far away does Oscar's grandfather live?

7. A banner has a length of 10 feet and an area of 7 square feet. What is the width of the banner?

8. Brady has three goldfish. This is $\frac{1}{5}$ times as many as Sam has. How many goldfish does Sam have?

9. Lucy has $\frac{1}{2}$ hour to decorate a dozen cupcakes for a bake sale. How much time can she spend on each cupcake?

10. If $\frac{1}{8}$ pound of uncooked rice makes one serving, how many servings are in a 15-pound bag of rice?

11. On Wednesday, 72 people watched the softball game. It rained on Friday, so only 18 people watched the game. The number of people who watched on Friday is how many times the number who watched on Wednesday?

▶ Solve Word Problems with Multiplication and Division

Show your work on your paper or in your journal.

Decide whether you need to multiply or divide. Then solve.

1. A turtle crawls 3 yards in an hour. How far will it crawl in 2 hours?

   How far will the turtle crawl in $\frac{1}{4}$ hour?

2. Emily has 2 tons of sand. She will move it by wheelbarrow to the garden. Her wheelbarrow holds $\frac{1}{10}$ ton. How many trips will she make?

3. Tawana has 3 pounds of nuts. She is using them to fill small bags with $\frac{1}{4}$ pound each. How many bags can she fill?

4. Roberto has a recipe that calls for 4 cups of flour. He wants to use only $\frac{1}{2}$ of the recipe today. How much flour will he need?

5. A picnic jug holds 1 gallon of lemonade. Each paper cup holds $\frac{1}{12}$ gallon. How many paper cups can be filled?

6. It rained on $\frac{2}{5}$ of all the days last month. On $\frac{1}{6}$ of these rainy days, there were thunderstorms. On what fraction of the days last month were there thunderstorms?

Use Activity Workbook page 40.

VOCABULARY
dividend
divisor
quotient

► Generalize Results

In the equations below, a and b are whole numbers greater than 1. $\frac{n}{d}$ is a fraction less than 1. $\frac{1}{d}$ is a unit fraction. Answer the questions about the equations.

Parts of a Division Problem

$$4 \div \frac{1}{3} = 12$$

dividend   divisor   quotient

Multiplication

7. $a \cdot b = c$

    Will c be greater than or less than a? _____ Why?

8. $a \cdot \frac{n}{d} = c$

    Will c be greater than or less than a? _____ Why?

Division

9. $a \div b = c$

    Will c be greater than or less than a? _____ Why?

10. $a \div \frac{1}{d} = c$

    Will c be greater than or less than a? _____ Why?

**Circle the problem with the greater answer.
Do not try to calculate the answer.**

11. $4,826 \cdot 581$ $4,826 \div 581$

12. $347 \cdot \frac{1}{72}$ $347 \div \frac{1}{72}$

Distinguish Multiplication from Division

▶ Predict the Size of the Result

Show your work on your paper or in your journal.

Decide what operation to use, predict the size of the result, then solve the problem.

13. Lucy spends 4 hours a week babysitting. Her sister Lily spends $\frac{7}{8}$ as much time babysitting. Does Lily babysit for more or less than 4 hours?

    Now find the exact amount of time Lily babysits.

14. Yoshi has a rope 30 feet long. He must cut it into pieces that are each $\frac{1}{4}$-foot long. Will he get more or fewer than 30 pieces?

    Now find the exact number of pieces Yoshi will get.

15. Carlos can throw a ball 14 yards. His friend Raul can throw $\frac{3}{7}$ of that distance. Is Raul's throw longer or shorter than 14 yards?

    Now find the exact length of Raul's throw.

16. An apple orchard covers 12 acres. There is a watering spout for every $\frac{1}{4}$ acre. Are there more or fewer than 12 watering spouts?

    Now find the exact number of watering spouts in the orchard.

▶ What's the Error?

Dear Math Students,

I have to divide 5 cups in half for a recipe.
Here's what I did:

$$5 \div \frac{1}{2} = 5 \cdot \frac{2}{1} = 10$$

I know I did the division correctly, but my
answer should be less than 5, not more. Can
you explain my mistake and help me fix it?

Your friend,
Puzzled Penguin

17. Write a response to Puzzled Penguin.

▶ Summarize Fraction Operations

18. You have just won a prize on a new quiz
show called *Quick Thinking.* The prize will
be *n* album downloads from an online
music store. You have a chance to change
your prize if you think you can make it
better. The screen shows the choices you
have. Which will you choose?

19. Suppose $n = 6$. How many albums have you won?

20. Suppose $n = 12$. How many albums have you won?

21. Discuss what you have learned about the size
of the answers when you mulitiply and divide by whole
numbers and by fractions.

► Choose the Operation

Decide what operation to use. Then solve.

1. Hala can ride her bike $7\frac{1}{2}$ miles in an hour. How far will she ride in 3 hours? How far will she ride in $\frac{1}{3}$ of an hour?

2. Eryn's pet rabbit eats $\frac{1}{12}$ pound of food every day. If Eryn buys rabbit food in 5-pound bags, how many days does one bag of rabbit food last?

3. Mr. Dayton uses 8 cups of flour to make three identical loaves of bread. How much flour is in each loaf?

4. Jonathan can throw a baseball $10\frac{1}{3}$ yards. His brother Joey can throw a baseball $13\frac{1}{12}$ yards. How much farther can Joey throw the ball?

5. Kim bought $\frac{3}{8}$ pound of sunflower seeds and $\frac{3}{16}$ pound of thistle seed for her bird feeder. How much seed did she buy in all?

6. Casandra's fish bowl holds $\frac{9}{10}$ gallon of water. It is now $\frac{2}{3}$ full. How much water is in the bowl?

► Predict and Solve

7. Marcus plays basketball for 9 hours each week. His friend Luis spends $\frac{5}{6}$ as much time playing basketball. Who plays more basketball?

   How much time does Luis spend playing basketball?

8. Stacey's long jump was 10 feet. That is $\frac{5}{6}$ foot longer than Ron's long jump. Did Ron jump more or less than 10 feet?

   How long was Ron's jump?

Show your work on your paper or in your journal.

► Practice Fraction Operations

Write the answer in simplest form.

9. $7 \div \frac{1}{3} =$ _____

10. $1\frac{5}{12} + 2\frac{5}{8} =$ _____

11. $\frac{1}{8} + \frac{5}{6} =$ _____

12. $\frac{4}{9} \cdot 8 =$ _____

13. $\frac{4}{7} - \frac{1}{3} =$ _____

14. $9 \div 10 =$ _____

15. $2\frac{3}{5} - 2\frac{6}{35} =$ _____

16. $\frac{2}{5} \cdot 5\frac{1}{2} =$ _____

17. $\frac{1}{6} + \frac{2}{9} =$ _____

18. $3\frac{1}{3} - 1\frac{3}{4} =$ _____

19. $1\frac{7}{8} \cdot 3\frac{2}{5} =$ _____

20. $\frac{1}{9} \div 3 =$ _____

Solve.

21. Mr. Jones's students recorded the number of hours they slept last night to the nearest quarter hour. The results are shown on this line plot.

Hours Slept

a. What is the range of values for the data (the difference between the greatest value and the least value)?

b. Six students slept $8\frac{1}{2}$ hours. What total number of hours do these six values represent?

c. Olivia said, "The longest time value is $1\frac{1}{2}$ times the shortest time value." Is she correct? Explain.

► **Math and Marching Bands**

The musicians in a marching band play many different kinds of musical instruments. Each type of instrument represents a part of the whole, which is all of the instruments in the band.

The circle graph below shows the fraction of all of the instruments in a school marching band that are bass drums.

bass drum
$\frac{1}{4}$

Show your work on your paper or in your journal.

Solve. Use the circle graph above.

1. The marching band has 15 bass drums. How many instruments altogether are in the band?

► Math and Marching Bands (continued)

Solve. Use the circle graph.

2. How many instruments of each kind are in the band?

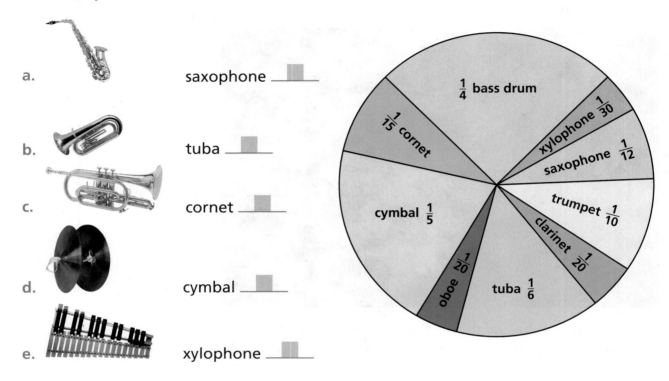

a. saxophone _____

b. tuba _____

c. cornet _____

d. cymbal _____

e. xylophone _____

3. The total number of clarinets and oboes is the same as the number of what other instrument?

4. Suppose the number of xylophones was doubled and the number of cornets was halved.

   a. In simplest form, what fraction of all of the instruments in the band would the new number of xylophones represent?

   b. In simplest form, what fraction of all of the instruments in the band would the new number of cornets represent?

   c. In simplest form, what fraction represents all of the *other* instruments in the band?

Use the Activity Workbook Unit Test on pages 41–42.

▶ Vocabulary

Choose the best term from the box.

1. To calculate $3\frac{3}{4} \cdot \frac{2}{3}$, first rewrite the

   _____ as a fraction. **(Lessons 3-6)**

2. In the equation $4 \div \frac{1}{3} = 12$, the number $\frac{1}{3}$ is a(n)

   _____. **(Lessons 3-10)**

3. The _____ tells us that $\frac{4}{7} \cdot \frac{5}{12} = \frac{5}{12} \cdot \frac{4}{7}$.

▶ Concepts and Skills

4. Three pounds of nuts are shared equally among 4 people. Explain why each person gets $\frac{3}{4}$ pound. Write a division equation to show this sharing situation. **(Lesson 3-10)**

5. Explain how this diagram models $\frac{2}{5} \cdot 3$. Then give the product. **(Lesson 3-3)**

Without multiplying, tell whether the product will be greater than, less than, or equal to the second factor. (Write >, <, or =.) (Lesson 3-9)

6. $\frac{10}{9} \cdot \frac{15}{32} = x$

   $x \bigcirc \frac{15}{32}$

7. $\frac{5}{6} \cdot 11 = x$

   $x \bigcirc 11$

8. $\frac{21}{21} \cdot \frac{7}{8} = x$

   $x \bigcirc \frac{7}{8}$

Solve. (Lessons 3-1 through 3-7)

9. $3 \div \frac{1}{5} = $ ▨

10. $\frac{3}{4} \cdot \frac{5}{7} = $ ▨

11. $8 \div 5 = $ ▨

12. $\frac{15}{32} \cdot \frac{16}{25} = $ ▨

13. $\frac{5}{8} \cdot 6 = $ ▨

14. $1\frac{1}{3} \cdot 1\frac{3}{5} = $ ▨

15. $9 \cdot \frac{2}{3} = $ ▨

16. $3 \cdot 2\frac{3}{8} = $ ▨

17. $\frac{1}{3} \div 7 = $ ▨

▶ Problem Solving

Solve. (Lessons 3-2 through 3-6 and 3-8 through 3-14)

18. The school cook made 30 pounds of potato salad for the school picnic. How many servings is this if each serving is $\frac{1}{4}$ pound?

19. Of the stamps in Malee's collection, $\frac{12}{35}$ are from Asia. Of these Asian stamps, $\frac{5}{16}$ are from Thailand. What fraction of Malee's stamps are from Thailand?

20. **Extended Response** A rectangular sign has a length of $3\frac{1}{2}$ feet and a width of $1\frac{1}{8}$ feet.

   a. Will the area of the sign be greater or less than $3\frac{1}{2}$ square feet? How do you know?

   b. What is the area of the sign?

Dear Family,

Unit 4 of *Math Expressions* introduces students to multiplying with multidigit numbers using models and different recording methods. The main goal of this unit is to develop skills in multiplying with whole numbers and decimal numbers. Some additional goals are:

• to solve real world application problems;

• to understand patterns in the number of zeros in the product when multiplying a number by 10, 100, or 1,000;

• to use estimation to check the reasonableness of answers;

• to understand and use exponents to denote powers of 10.

Your child will learn and practice techniques such as Place Value Sections, Expanded Notation, and Shift Patterns to gain speed and accuracy in multidigit and decimal multiplication. Money examples will be used in multiplication with decimals.

Share with your family the Family Letter on Activity Workbook page 43.

Place Value Sections

81×14	80	$+$	1
10	$80 \times 10 = 800$		$1 \times 10 = 10$
$+$			
4	$80 \times 4 = 320$		$1 \times 4 = 4$

Expanded Form

$$81 = 80 + 1$$
$$\times\ 14 = 10 + 4$$
$$80 \times 10 = 800$$
$$80 \times\ \ 4 = 320$$
$$1 \times 10 = \ \ 10$$
$$1 \times\ \ 4 = \ \ \ \ 4$$
$$1{,}134$$

Throughout Unit 4, your child will solve real world problems that require multidigit multiplication as well as using rounding and mental math to estimate products.

If you have any questions, please call or write to me.

Sincerely,
Your child's teacher

COMMON CORE This unit includes the Common Core Standards for Mathematical Content for the Number System, CC.5.NBT.1, CC.5.NBT.2, CC.5.NBT.3a, CC.5.NBT.4, CC.5.NBT.5, CC.5.NBT.7, and all Mathematical Practices.

Dear Family,

La Unidad 4 de *Math Expressions* introduce a los estudiantes a la multiplicación con números de varios dígitos por medio del uso de modelos y varios métodos de anotación. El objetivo principal de la unidad es desarrollar destrezas para multiplicar con números enteros y decimales. Algunos objetivos adicionales son:

• resolver problemas con aplicaciones a la vida diaria;

• reconocer patrones en el número de ceros en el producto al multiplicar un número por 10, 100 ó 1,000;

• usar la estimación para comprobar que las respuestas sean razonables;

• reconocer y usar exponentes para indicar potencias de 10.

Su niño aprenderá y practicará técnicas tales como Secciones de valor posicional, Notación extendida y Patrones de desplazamiento, para adquirir rapidez y exactitud en la multiplicación con números de varios dígitos y decimales. En las multiplicaciones con decimales se usarán ejemplos de dinero.

Muestra a tu familia la Carta a la familia de la página 44 del Cuaderno de actividades y trabajo.

Secciones de valor posicional

81 × 14	80	+	1
10	80 × 10 = 800		$1 \times 10 = 10$
+			
4	80 × 4 = 320		$1 \times 4 = 4$

Notación extendida

$$81 = 80 + 1$$
$$\times\ 14 = 10 + 4$$
$$80 \times 10 = 800$$
$$80 \times 4 = 320$$
$$1 \times 10 = 10$$
$$1 \times 4 = 4$$
$$1,134$$

Durante el transcurso de la Unidad 4 su niño resolverá problemas de la vida diaria que requieran el uso de la multiplicación de números de varios dígitos, del redondeo, y del cálculo mental para estimar productos.

Si tiene alguna duda o algún comentario, por favor comuníquese conmigo.

Atentamente,
El maestro su niño

COMMON CORE

Esta unidad incluye los Common Core Standards for Mathematical Content for the Number System, CC.5.NBT.1, CC.5.NBT.2, CC.5.NBT.3a, CC.5.NBT.4, CC.5.NBT.5, CC.5.NBT.7, and all Mathematical Practices.

VOCABULARY
shift

▶ Shifts with Whole Numbers

Jordan earns $243 a week. The money is shown at the right. Answer the questions about how much he will earn over time.

Jordan's Weekly Earnings

$ ____ ____ ____ , 2   4   3

× 1

1 × $243 = $243

_____

When you multiply by 10, the digits shift by one place to the left.

1. After 10 weeks, how much will Jordan have earned?

After 10 Weeks

$ ____ ____ 2 , 4   3   0

× 10

10 × $243 = $2,430

2. What happens to each $1-bill when it is multiplied by 10?

3. What happens to each other bill when it is multiplied by 10?

4. When you multiply by 10, does each digit **shift** to the right or left?

5. How many places does each digit shift?

6. After 100 weeks, how much will Jordan have earned?

After 100 Weeks

	$2	4		3	0	0

7. What happens to each $1-bill when it is multiplied by 100?

× 100

10 × 10 × $243 = $24,300

8. What happens to each digit when it is multiplied by 100?

9. When you multiply by 100, does each digit shift to the right or left?

10. How many places does each digit shift?

11. After 1,000 weeks, how much will Jordan have earned?

After 1,000 Weeks

$	2	4	3	,	0	0	0

12. What happens to each $1-bill when it is multiplied by 1,000?

× 1,000

13. What happens to each digit when it is multiplied by 1,000?

10 × 10 × 10 × $243 = $243,000

14. When you multiply by 1,000, does each digit shift to the right or left?

15. How many places does each digit shift?

Shift Patterns in Multiplication

► See the Shift in Motion

Isabel earns $325 a week. Three students can show how the digits shift at the board when we multiply her earnings.

Complete each exercise.

16. Suppose Isabel works for 10 weeks. Find her earnings.

____ ____ ____ , $ 3   2   5 | × 10 ⟩ ____ ____ $ 3 , __2__ __5__ __0__

$325 shifts ____ place(s) to the ____. It becomes 10 times as great.

17. Suppose Isabel works for 100 weeks. Find her earnings.

____ ____ ____ , $ 3   2   5 | × 100 ⟩ ____ $ 3 __2__ , __5__ __0__ __0__

$325 shifts ____ places to the ____. It becomes 100 times as great.

18. Suppose Isabel works for 1,000 weeks. Find her earnings.

____ ____ ____ , $ 3   2   5 | × 1,000 ⟩ $ 3 __2__ __5__ , __0__ __0__ __0__

$325 shifts ____ places to the ____. It becomes 1,000 times as great.

Complete each exercise.

19. $567 \times 10 =$ ▨

20. $38 \times 1{,}000 =$ ▨

21. $912 \times 100 =$ ▨

22. $700 \times 10 =$ ▨

23. The Skyway Express train travels about 800 miles a day. How far does it travel in 10 days?

24. Since there are 30 days in April, about how far will the train travel during the month of April?

► Shifts with Decimal Amounts

It costs $0.412 (41 and $\frac{2}{10}$ cents) for a
factory to make a Red Phantom Marble.
The money is shown here.

Cost of a Red Phantom Marble

**Answer each question about the cost of making different
numbers of Red Phantom Marbles.**

25. How much does it cost to make
10 Red Phantom Marbles?

10 Red Phantom Marbles

26. What happens to each coin when
it is multiplied by 10?

27. What happens to each digit?

28. When you multiply by 10, does each
digit shift to the right or left?

29. How many places does each digit shift?

30. How much does it cost to make
100 Red Phantom Marbles?

100 Red Phantom Marbles

31. What happens to each coin
when you multiply by 100?

$ ____ \underline{\ 4\ } \quad \underline{\ 1\ } . \underline{\ 2\ } \quad \underline{\ 0\ } \quad ____

× 100

32. What happens to each digit?

$100 × \$0.412 = \$41.20$

33. When you multiply by 100, does each digit
shift to the right or left?

34. How many places does each digit shift?

35. How much does it cost to make
1,000 Red Phantom Marbles?

1,000 Red Phantom Marbles

36. What happens to each coin
when you multiply by 1,000?

$ \underline{\ 4\ } \quad \underline{\ 1\ } \quad \underline{\ 2\ } . \underline{\ 0\ } \quad \underline{\ 0\ } \quad ____

× 1,000

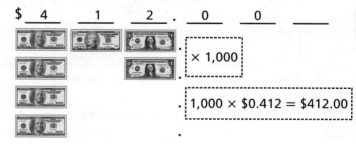

37. What happens to each digit?

$1,000 × \$0.412 = \$412.00$

38. When you multiply by 1,000, does each
digit shift to the right or left?

39. How many places does each digit shift?

► Patterns in Multiplying with Zeros

Discuss patterns you see across each row and down each column. Then state a generalization for multiplying numbers with zeros.

×	3	30	300	3,000
2	**a.** $2 \times 3 = 6$	**b.** 2×30 $= 2 \times 3 \times 10$ $= 6 \times 10$ $= 60$	**c.** 2×300 $= 2 \times 3 \times 100$ $= 6 \times 100$ $= 600$	**d.** $2 \times 3,000$ $= 2 \times 3 \times 1,000$ $= 6 \times 1,000$ $= 6,000$
20	**e.** 20×3 $= 2 \times 10 \times 3$ $= 6 \times 10$ $= 60$	**f.** 20×30 $= 2 \times 10 \times 3$ $\times 10$ $= 6 \times 100$ $= 600$	**g.** 20×300 $= 2 \times 10 \times 3$ $\times 100$ $= 6 \times 1,000$ $= 6,000$	**h.** $20 \times 3,000$ $= 2 \times 10 \times 3$ $\times 1,000$ $= 6 \times 10,000$ $= 60,000$
200	**i.** 200×3 $= 2 \times 100 \times 3$ $= 6 \times 100$ $= 600$	**j.** 200×30 $= 2 \times 100 \times 3$ $\times 10$ $= 6 \times 1,000$ $= 6,000$	**k.** 200×300 $= 2 \times 100 \times 3$ $\times 100$ $= 6 \times 10,000$ $= 60,000$	**l.** $200 \times 3,000$ $= 2 \times 100 \times 3$ $\times 1,000$ $= 6 \times 100,000$ $= 600,000$
2,000	**m.** $2,000 \times 3$ $= 2 \times 1,000 \times 3$ $= 6 \times 1,000$ $= 6,000$	**n.** $2,000 \times 30$ $= 2 \times 1,000 \times 3$ $\times 10$ $= 6 \times 10,000$ $= 60,000$	**o.** $2,000 \times 300$ $= 2 \times 1,000 \times 3$ $\times 100$ $= 6 \times 100,000$ $= 600,000$	**p.** $2,000 \times 3,000$ $= 2 \times 1,000 \times 3$ $\times 1,000$ $= 6 \times 1,000,000$ $= 6,000,000$

Solve.

40.	41.	42.	43.	44.
$\begin{array}{r} 60 \\ \times\ \ 3 \\ \hline \end{array}$	$\begin{array}{r} 60 \\ \times\ 30 \\ \hline \end{array}$	$\begin{array}{r} 600 \\ \times\ \ 30 \\ \hline \end{array}$	$\begin{array}{r} 600 \\ \times\ 300 \\ \hline \end{array}$	$\begin{array}{r} 6,000 \\ \times\ \ \ 30 \\ \hline \end{array}$

▶ Powers of Ten

Expressions with repeated factors such as $10 \times 10 \times 10$ can be written by using a base with an exponent. The **base** is the number that is used as the repeated factor. The **exponent** is a number that tell how many times the base is used as a factor.

$$1{,}000 = 10 \times 10 \times 10 = 10^3$$

exponent

3 factors

base

When you represent a number using a base and an exponent, you are using **exponential form**.

Exponential form: 10^3

Word form: ten raised to the third power or
the third **power of ten**

Write each expression as repeated multiplication and solve.

45. $10^2 =$ _____ = ____

46. $10^5 =$ _____

= _____

47. $10^4 =$ _____

= _____

48. $10^1 =$ _____ = ____

Use an exponent to write each repeated multiplication.

49. $5 \times 10 \times 10 =$ ▇

50. $3 \times 10 \times 10 \times 10 \times 10 =$ ▇

51. $9 \times 10 \times 10 \times 10 =$ ▇

52. $2 \times 10 =$ ▇

53. $7 \times 10 \times 10 \times 10 \times 10 \times 10$

= ▇

54. $1 \times 10 \times 10 =$ ▇

Use Activity
Workbook page 45.

► Multiply a Whole Number by a Power of Ten

Multiply 3 by powers of ten. Look for a pattern.

$3 \times 10^1 = 3 \times 10 = 30$

$3 \times 10^2 = 3 \times 10 \times 10 = $ ■

$3 \times 10^3 = 3 \times 10 \times 10 \times 10 = $ ■

$30 \times 10^3 = (3 \times 10) \times 10 \times 10 \times 10 = $ ■

55. What pattern do you see?

Find the value.

56. $1 \times 10^4 = $ ■

57. $2 \times 10^3 = $ ■

58. $62 \times 10^2 = $ ■

Complete the pattern.

59. $7 \times 10^1 = 7 \times 10 = $ ____

$7 \times 10^2 = 7 \times 100 = $ ____

$7 \times 10^3 = 7 \times 1,000 = $ ____

$7 \times 10^4 = 7 \times 10,000 = $ ____

60. $9 \times 10^1 = $ ____ $ = 90$

$9 \times 10^2 = $ ____ $ = 900$

$9 \times 10^3 = $ ____ $ = 9,000$

$9 \times 10^4 = $ ____ $ = 90,000$

61. $65 \times 10^1 = 65 \times 10 = $ ____

$65 \times 10^2 = 65 \times 100 = $ ____

$65 \times 10^3 = 65 \times 1,000 = $ ____

$65 \times 10^4 = 65 \times 10,000 = $ ____

62. $523 \times 10^1 = $ ____ $ = 5,230$

$523 \times 10^2 = 523 \times 100 = $ ____

$523 \times 10^3 = $ ____ $ = 523,000$

$523 \times 10^4 = 523 \times 10,000 = $ ____

63. $14 \times 10^1 = 14 \times 10 = $ ____

$14 \times 10^2 = 14 \times 100 = $ ____

$14 \times 10^3 = 14 \times 1,000 = $ ____

$14 \times 10^4 = 14 \times 10,000 = $ ____

64. $108 \times 10^1 = $ ____ $ = 1,080$

$108 \times 10^2 = 108 \times 100 = $ ____

$108 \times 10^3 = $ ____ $ = 108,000$

$108 \times 10^4 = 108 \times 10,000 = $ ____

Use Activity
Workbook page 46.

▶ Patterns with Fives

Dear Math Students,

I know that when you multiply two numbers together, the product has the same number of zeros as the two factors. For example, 60 × 20 is 1,200. There are two zeros in the factors (60 and 20) and two zeros in the product (1,200).

I am confused about one thing. I know that 50 × 2 is 100, and I am quite sure that 50 × 4 is 200. In these two problems, there is only one zero in the factors, but there are **two** zeros in the product. The pattern I learned does not seem to be true in these cases.

Did I make a mistake somewhere?

Thank you.
Puzzled Penguin

1. Write an answer to Puzzled Penguin.

2. Find each product to complete the chart below. One factor in each problem contains a 5. Discuss the patterns you see for the number of zeros in each product. How does the number of zeros in the product relate to the number of zeros in the factors?

5 × 20	=	5 × 2 × 10	=	10 × 10	= ▨
50 × 40	=	5 × 10 × 4 × 10	=	20 × 100	= ▨
50 × 600	=	5 × 10 × 6 × 100	=	30 × 1,000	= ▨
500 × 800	=	5 × 100 × 8 × 100	=	40 × 10,000	= ▨

Use Activity
Workbook page 47.

3. Find each product to complete the chart below. Again, one factor in each problem contains a 5. How does the number of zeros in the product relate to the number of zeros in the factors?

5×30	=	$5 \times 3 \times 10$	=	15×10	=	▮
50×50	=	$5 \times 10 \times 5 \times 10$	=	25×100	=	▮
50×700	=	$5 \times 10 \times 7 \times 100$	=	$35 \times 1,000$	=	▮
500×900	=	$5 \times 100 \times 9 \times 100$	=	$45 \times 10,000$	=	▮

4. Explain why the product sometimes has an "extra" zero.

▶ Solve Fives-Pattern Problems

Decide how many zeros there will be. Then solve.

5. $\begin{array}{r} 80 \\ \times\ 5 \\ \hline \end{array}$
6. $\begin{array}{r} 70 \\ \times\ 5 \\ \hline \end{array}$
7. $\begin{array}{r} 90 \\ \times\ 50 \\ \hline \end{array}$
8. $\begin{array}{r} 60 \\ \times\ 50 \\ \hline \end{array}$

Write an equation. Then solve.

9. Ernesto and his sister Dora are playing a computer game. Ernesto has earned 200 points so far. His sister has earned 50 times as many points. How many points has Dora earned?

10. Mount Katahdin is the tallest mountain in Maine. It is about 5,000 feet tall. Mount McKinley is the tallest mountain in the United States. It is four times as tall as Mount Katahdin. About how tall is Mount McKinley?

Use Activity Workbook page 48.

VOCABULARY
Place Value Sections
partial products

▶ **Solve with Place Value Sections**

Think about finding the area of this rectangle (*Area = length × width*). It would be difficult to find 43 × 67 in one step, but if you broke the rectangle into smaller **Place Value Sections**, then you could do it.

When you multiply larger numbers, you often need to break the problem into smaller parts. The products of these smaller parts are called **partial products**. After you find all the partial products, you can add them together.

1. A flower garden is 67 inches long and 43 inches wide. What is the area of the garden? Explain how Place Value Sections are used to solve the problem below.

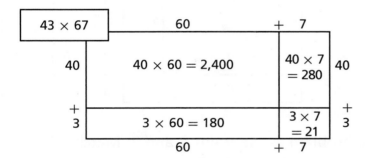

2. A theater has 39 rows of seats. Each row has 54 seats. How many seats are in the theater? Use Place Value Sections to solve the multiplication problem below.

Use Activity
Workbook page 49.

VOCABULARY
Expanded Notation

► Numerical Methods for Multiplication

Look at the **Expanded Notation** method of solving 43 × 67 below.
Diagrams A and B both show the Expanded Notation method.
Diagram B only shows the results of the steps.

3. How is this method like the Place Value Sections? How is it different?

4. The rectangle above shows the same problem as Diagrams A and B. Match each section (a, b, c, d) to the 4 partial products shown in the Expanded Notation method above.

Solve. Use any method you like.

5. There are 32 cattle cars on today's train to Detroit. Each car holds 28 cows. How many cows are on the train?

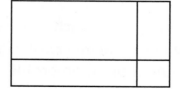

6. Mr. Brooks is planning to carpet his office. The office is 21 feet long and 52 feet wide. How much carpet does he need if he carpets the entire room?

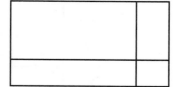

The Area Model for Multiplication

Use Activity Workbook page 50.

▶ Methods for Two-Digit Multiplication

Look at the multiplication problem shown here. It is solved with another place value method called **Place Value Rows**.

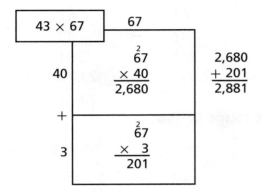

1. Explain the steps of the Place Value Rows method.

2. How is the Place Value Rows method alike and different from the Place Value Sections method?

Use the Place Value Rows method to solve each problem.

3.

28 × 34

4.

59 × 73

VOCABULARY
New Groups Below
Short Cut

Here, 43 × 67 is solved with a method we call the **Short Cut**.

Step 1	Step 2	Step 3	Step 4	Step 5	Step 6
²67	²67	²67	²²67	²²67	²²67
× 43	× 43	× 43	× 43	× 43	× 43
1	201	201	201	201	201
		0	80	2,680	2,680
					2,881

Here, 43 × 67 is solved with a method we call **New Groups Below**.

Step 1	Step 2	Step 3	Step 4	Step 5	Step 6
67	67	67	67	67	67
× 43	× 43	× 43	× 43	× 43	× 43
²1	¹²81	¹²81	¹²81	¹²81	¹²81
		0	²80	²²480	²²480
					¹2,881

5. **Discuss** How is the Short Cut method different from the New Groups Below method?

6. **Discuss** How is the Short Cut method like the Place Value Rows method? How is it different?

The Place Value Rows and Short Cut methods both make use of the Distributive Property.

In each, one factor is broken into two addends which are multiplied by the other factor.

$$67 \times 43 = 67(40 + 3)$$

$$= (67 \times 40) + (67 \times 3)$$

$$= (2,680) + (201)$$

$$= 2,881$$

7. Use another 2-digit by 2-digit multiplication problem to illustrate how to use the Distributive Property.

Multiply Two-Digit Numbers

▶ Discuss Multiplication Methods

Below are the four multiplication methods your class has tried. Discuss these questions about the methods.

7. How do the 4 partial products in the two top methods relate to the 2 partial products in the two bottom methods?

8. The Short Cut method starts with the ones. Could we do the other methods by starting with the ones? Explain why or why not.

Place Value Sections

43×67

	60	+ 7
40	$40 \times 60 = 2400$	$40 \times 7 = 280$
+ 3	$3 \times 60 = 180$	$3 \times 7 = 21$

40 ... 40
+3 ... +3
60 ... + 7

Expanded Notation

$$67 = 60 + 7$$
$$43 = 40 + 3$$
$$40 \times 60 = 2{,}400$$
$$40 \times 7 = 280$$
$$3 \times 60 = 180$$
$$3 \times 7 = 21$$
$$2{,}881$$

Place Value Rows

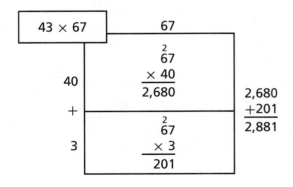

43×67

	67
40	$\overset{2}{67}$ $\times\ 40$ = 2,680
+ 3	$\overset{2}{67}$ $\times\ 3$ = 201

2,680
+201
2,881

Short Cut

New Groups Above

$$\overset{2}{\underset{}{\overset{2}{67}}}$$
$$\times\ 43$$
$$201$$
$$2{,}680$$
$$2{,}881$$

New Groups Below

$$67$$
$$\times\ 43$$
$$\overset{1\ 2}{81}$$
$$\overset{2\ 2}{480}$$
$$2{,}881$$

Solve.

9. $\begin{array}{r} 94 \\ \times\ 36 \\ \hline \end{array}$

10. $\begin{array}{r} 73 \\ \times\ 45 \\ \hline \end{array}$

11. $\begin{array}{r} 69 \\ \times\ 82 \\ \hline \end{array}$

PATH to FLUENCY Practice Multiplying Multidigit Numbers

Solve. Use any method.

12.	42 × 5	13.	37 × 9	14.	742 × 4	15.	5,553 × 2
16.	204 × 6	17.	7,128 × 7	18.	54 × 3	19.	385 × 8
20.	24 × 15	21.	28 × 92	22.	54 × 47	23.	35 × 29
24.	27 × 29	25.	71 × 43	26.	63 × 85	27.	38 × 50
28.	83 × 83	29.	17 × 71	30.	44 × 55	31.	75 × 16

▶ Solve Real World Problems

Show your work on your paper or in your journal.

32. Max rode his bike 44 miles every week for 28 weeks. How many miles did he ride altogether?

33. Monique wants to cover a watercolor painting with glass. The painting is 25 inches long and 35 inches wide. What is the area of the glass needed for the painting?

PATH to FLUENCY **Practice Multiplying**

Multiply.

1. 54
    × 7

2. 508
    × 6

3. 945
    × 8

4. 2,786
    × 3

5. 643
    × 4

6. 5,433
    × 2

7. 1,079
    × 7

8. 400
    × 50

9. 49
    × 76

10. 65
     × 24

11. 40
     × 40

12. 53
     × 35

13. 27
     × 98

14. 33
     × 88

15. 71
     × 28

16. 92
     × 47

17. 21
     × 29

18. 47
     × 37

19. 44
     × 44

20. 54
     × 75

▶ **Solve Real World Problems**

Show your work on your paper or in your journal.

Solve.

21. Pascal wants to read 99 pages every week for 35 weeks.
How many pages will he have read by the end of that time?
How could he use mental math to find the solution?

22. Jenny's garden is 28 feet by 50 feet. What is the area of her
garden? How could she use mental math to find the area?

23. Padma has a dining room table whose top is 42 inches wide
and 72 inches long. What is the area of the top of her table?

24. The drama club is making punch to sell at the school play.
Each batch uses 64 fluid ounces of fruit juice. If they plan to
make 18 batches, how much fruit juice will they need?

Write an equation and then solve.

25. Tigers living in Siberia can have home ranges from 190 to
1,500 square miles depending on how plentiful their prey is.
If a tiger's range is in the shape of a rectangle that is 47 miles
wide by 29 miles long, what is the area of its home range?

26. Paul and John have a stamp collection. They keep their stamps
in an album that has 54 pages. There are 24 stamps on each
side of each page. How many stamps are in their collection?

Practice Multiplication

Use Activity Workbook page 51.

▶ Decimals in Money Situations

The Ruiz children had a yard sale. They sold some old toys. They made a table to show how many toys they sold and how much money they earned.

Number of Items	Item Price	Total Earned in Cents	Total Earned in Dollars
3 jump ropes	9 cents	3 × 9 cents = 27 cents	3 × $0.09 = $0.27
4 marbles	2 cents	4 × 2 cents = 8 cents	4 × $0.02 = $0.08
6 toy cars	12 cents	6 × 12 cents = 72 cents	6 × $0.12 = $0.72
5 puzzles	30 cents	5 × 30 cents = 150 cents	5 × $0.30 = $1.50

1. How did they know the number of decimal places in each product in the last column?

2. How much money did they earn in dollars?

Mia saves the change from her lunch money each day. She gets $0.34 in change, and she has been saving it for 26 days. Mia used the steps below to find how much money she has saved so far.

$$\$0.34 = \$0.30 + \$0.04$$
$$\times\ 26 =\ \ \ \ \ 20 +\ \ \ \ \ 6$$

Step 1	Multiply by the number in the ones place (6).	6 × $0.04 = 6 × 4 cents = 24 cents = $0.24 6 × $0.30 = 6 × 30 cents = 180 cents = $1.80
Step 2	Multiply by the number in the tens place (2 tens = 20).	20 × $0.04 = 20 × 4 cents = 80 cents = ▨ 20 × $0.30 = 20 × 30 cents = 60 dimes = ▨
Step 3	Add the partial products.	▨

3. How many decimal places are there in the decimal factor (0.34)? How many decimal places are there in the answer?

▶ Decimals in Money Situations (continued)

A bead factory spends $0.65 to make each crystal bead. The steps below show how Antonio finds the total amount the factory spends to make 222 crystal beads.

$0.65
× 222

Step 1	Multiply by the number in the ones place.	2 × $0.65 = ▦
Step 2	Multiply by the number in the tens place. (2 tens = 20; 1.30 shifts 1 place left.)	20 × $0.65 = ▦
Step 3	Multiply by the number in the hundreds place. (2 hundreds = 200; 1.30 shifts 2 places left.)	200 × $0.65 = ▦
Step 4	Add the partial products.	▦

4. How many decimal places are there in the decimal factor (0.65)? How many decimal places are there in the answer?

5. Describe the relationship between the number of decimal places you have seen in a decimal product and the number of decimal places in its decimal factor.

6. The owners of the Seven Seas Spice Company want to sell twice as much spice in the future as they do now. The table shows how much spice they sell in a week now and how much they want to sell in the future. Show how to get the answers by adding.

Cloves	0.3 ton	2 × 0.3 ton = 0.6 ton	because 0.3 + 0.3 = 0.6
Cinnamon	0.04 ton	2 × 0.04 ton = 0.08 ton	because 0.04 + ▦ = ▦
Ginger	0.07 ton	2 × 0.07 ton = 0.14 ton	because ▦ + ▦ = ▦
Pepper	0.6 ton	2 × 0.6 ton = 1.2 tons	because ▦ + ▦ = ▦

7. Look at the number of decimal places in each decimal factor and the number of decimal places in each product. What pattern do you see?

8. Is this the same pattern you saw in Problems 1–4?

▶ Practice Multiplying with Decimals

Find each product.

9. 0.8
    × 6

10. 0.3
    × 40

11. 0.05
    × 9

12. 0.14
    × 32

13. 0.43
    × 64

14. 0.27
    × 31

15. 0.7
    × 333

16. 0.2
    × 421

17. 0.11
    × 219

18. 0.67
    × 102

19. 1.03
    × 15

20. 2.15
    × 35

21. 3.25
    × 25

22. 6.01
    × 19

23. 2.03
    × 111

Solve.

24. Jesse bought 3 aquariums. Each holds 8.75 gallons of water. How many gallons of water will they hold altogether?

Show your work on your paper or in your journal.

25. Jesse wants to buy 24 angelfish. Each angelfish costs $2.35. What will be the total cost of the angelfish?

26. There are three goldfish in one of Jesse's aquariums. Gus is the smallest. He weighs only 0.98 ounce. Ella weighs 3 times as much as Gus. What is Ella's weight?

▶ Zero Patterns in Decimal Places

You have seen patterns in multiplying by multiples of 10.
You have seen patterns in multiplying by decimals. You can use
these two patterns together. The table below shows how you
can multiply decimals by whole numbers, using:
- ones, tens, and hundreds
- tenths, hundredths, and thousandths

x	0.3	0.03	0.003
2	2 × 0.3 = 2 × 3 × 0.1 = 6 × 0.1 = 0.6	2 × 0.03 = 2 × 3 × 0.01 = 6 × 0.01 = 0.06	2 × 0.003 = 2 × 3 × 0.001 = 6 × 0.001 = 0.006
20	20 × 0.3 = 2 × 10 × 3 × 0.1 = 60 × 0.1 = 6.0	20 × 0.03 = 2 × 10 × 3 × 0.01 = 60 × 0.01 = 0.60	20 × 0.003 = 2 × 10 × 3 × 0.001 = 60 × 0.001 = 0.060
200	200 × 0.3 = 2 × 100 × 3 × 0.1 = 600 × 0.1 = 60.0	200 × 0.03 = 2 × 100 × 3 × 0.01 = 600 × 0.01 = 6.00	200 × 0.003 = 2 × 100 × 3 × 0.001 = 600 × 0.001 = 0.600

Find each product using the method shown in the table above.

27. 4 × 0.2 = ▨

28. 5 × 0.6 = ▨

39. 40 × 0.07 = ▨

30. 300 × 0.3 = ▨

31. 200 × 0.08 = ▨

► **Shifts with Decimals**

Leon earns $213 a month. The money is shown here. He will save some of it every month.

Leon's Earnings

$2 ___ 1 ___ 3 . ____ ____

Answer the questions about the different savings plans.

1. If he saves 0.1 of his earnings, how much will he save each month?

Save 0.1 Each Month

____ $2 ___ 1 . ___ 3 ___ 0

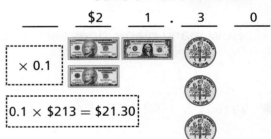

2. What happens to the value of each bill?

3. What happens to the value of each digit?

4. When you multiply by 0.1, does each digit shift to the right or left?

5. How many places does each digit shift?

▶ Shifts with Decimals (continued)

6. If he saves 0.01 of his earnings, how much will he save each month?

Save 0.01 Each Month

$ ____ ____ 2 . 1 3

7. What happens to the value of each bill?

× 0.01

0.01 × $213 = $2.13

8. What happens to the value of each digit?

9. When you multiply by 0.01, does each digit shift to the right or left?

10. How many places does each digit shift?

▶ What's the Error?

Dear Math Students,

Today I went to the bank to deposit $345.00. When I told the banker this was 0.1 of $34.50, he told me that I'd made a mistake.

Can you tell me what I did wrong?

Your friend,
Puzzled Penguin

11. Write a response to Puzzled Penguin.

Use Activity
Workbook page 53.

▶ See the Shift in Motion

Marla earns $324 a month. She will save some of her money every month. Three students can show how the digits shift at the board.

$$\underline{3} \quad \underline{2} \quad \underline{4} \quad . \quad \underline{} \quad \underline{} \quad \underline{}$$

Complete each exercise.

12. Suppose Marla saves 0.1 of $324 every month.

$\$3 \quad \underline{2} \quad \underline{4} \quad . \quad \underline{} \quad \underline{} \quad \boxed{\times 0.1} \quad \underline{} \quad \$3 \quad \underline{2} \quad . \quad \underline{4} \quad \underline{0}$

$324 shifts \underline{} place(s) to the \underline{}. It becomes \underline{} as much.

13. Suppose Marla saves 0.01 of $324 every month.

$\$3 \quad \underline{2} \quad \underline{4} \quad . \quad \underline{} \quad \underline{} \quad \boxed{\times 0.01} \quad \underline{} \quad \underline{} \quad \$3 \quad . \quad \underline{2} \quad \underline{4}$

$324 shifts \underline{} place(s) to the \underline{}. It becomes \underline{} as much.

Multiply and discuss the pattern.

14. $24 \times 1 = \blacksquare$

$24 \times 0.1 = \blacksquare$

$24 \times 0.01 = \blacksquare$

15. $689 \times 1 = \blacksquare$

$689 \times 0.1 = \blacksquare$

$689 \times 0.01 = \blacksquare$

16. $42 \times 0.01 = \blacksquare$

17. $339 \times 0.01 = \blacksquare$

18. $12 \times 0.1 = \blacksquare$

19. $59 \times 0.01 = \blacksquare$

20. $837 \times 0.01 = \blacksquare$

21. $672 \times 0.1 = \blacksquare$

22. Chris has $0.10. Katie has 10 times as much money as Chris. How much money does Katie have?

23. Brian gets $15.00 to mow the lawn. He saves 0.1 of his earnings. How much money does Brian save?

24. Juliet earned $24 this week. She wants to save 100 times as much as she earned this week. How much money does she want to save?

25. Gerard has 0.01 as much money as William. William has $125.00. How much money does Gerard have?

▶ Shifts When Both Factors Are Decimals

Multiply by one tenth. Think about what it means to take one tenth of another part. You can think about money.

26. $0.1 \times 0.4 =$ _____ Think: What is one tenth of one tenth? Then, what is one tenth of four tenths?

27. $0.1 \times 0.04 =$ _____ Think: What is one tenth of one hundredth? Then, what is one tenth of four hundredths?

28. How many places did the 4 shift each time you multiplied? _____ In which direction?

29. Look at your answers. What pattern do you see in the number of decimal places in the products? How is it related to the number of places in the two factors?

Multiply by one hundredth. Think about what it means to take one hundredth of another part.

30. $0.01 \times 4 =$ _____ Think: What is one hundredth of one? Then, what is one hundredth of four?

31. $0.01 \times 0.4 =$ _____ Think: What is one hundredth of one tenth? Then, what is one hundredth of four tenths?

32. How many places did the 4 shift each time you multiplied? _____ In which direction?

33. Look at your answers. What pattern do you see in the number of decimal places in the products? How is it related to the number of places in the two factors?

Use Activity
Workbook page 54.

▶ Shifts When Both Factors Are Decimals (continued)

34. How could you express the generalization about the number of decimal places in the product when you multiply a decimal number by another decimal number? Is it the same as the generalization for multiplying a decimal number by a whole number?

35. To multiply by 2 tenths or 2 hundredths, you could think of 2 tenths as 2×0.1 and 2 hundredths as 2×0.01.

$0.2 \times 0.4 = (2 \times \underline{\quad\quad}) \times 0.4 = 2 \times (0.1 \times 0.4) = 2 \times 0.04 = \underline{\quad\quad}$

$0.02 \times 0.4 = (2 \times \underline{\quad\quad}) \times 0.4 = 2 \times (0.01 \times 0.4) = 2 \times 0.004 = \underline{\quad\quad}$

Is your generalization about the number of decimal places in the product still true?

Use the shift pattern to solve each multiplication. Check to see if the generalization works.

36. $0.2 \times 0.4 = \blacksquare$ **37.** $0.2 \times 0.04 = \blacksquare$

38. $2 \times 0.4 = \blacksquare$ **39.** $0.02 \times 0.4 = \blacksquare$

40.
$$\begin{array}{r} 0.4 \\ \times\ 6 \\ \hline \end{array}$$

41.
$$\begin{array}{r} 0.04 \\ \times\ 6 \\ \hline \end{array}$$

42.
$$\begin{array}{r} 0.4 \\ \times\ 0.6 \\ \hline \end{array}$$

43.
$$\begin{array}{r} 0.4 \\ \times\ 0.06 \\ \hline \end{array}$$

44.
$$\begin{array}{r} 0.05 \\ \times\ 3 \\ \hline \end{array}$$

45.
$$\begin{array}{r} 0.13 \\ \times\ 2 \\ \hline \end{array}$$

46.
$$\begin{array}{r} 1.2 \\ \times\ 3 \\ \hline \end{array}$$

47.
$$\begin{array}{r} 0.2 \\ \times\ 0.6 \\ \hline \end{array}$$

► Shifts When Both Factors Are Decimals (continued)

Using the generalization you just discovered, solve each multiplication.

48. $0.3 \times 0.4 =$ ▓

49. $0.3 \times 0.04 =$ ▓

50. $0.03 \times 0.4 =$ ▓

51. $3 \times 0.4 =$ ▓

52. $\begin{array}{r} 0.05 \\ \times\ 5 \\ \hline \end{array}$

53. $\begin{array}{r} 0.9 \\ \times\ 0.3 \\ \hline \end{array}$

54. $\begin{array}{r} 0.07 \\ \times\ 0.3 \\ \hline \end{array}$

55. $\begin{array}{r} 0.4 \\ \times\ 0.08 \\ \hline \end{array}$

56. $\begin{array}{r} 0.4 \\ \times\ 5 \\ \hline \end{array}$

57. $\begin{array}{r} 0.3 \\ \times\ 1.3 \\ \hline \end{array}$

58. $\begin{array}{r} 0.2 \\ \times\ 0.26 \\ \hline \end{array}$

59. $\begin{array}{r} 0.7 \\ \times\ 4.2 \\ \hline \end{array}$

Solve.

Show your work on your paper or in your journal.

60. Benjamin bought 6.2 pounds of rice. Each pound cost $0.90. How much did he spend on rice?

61. Sabrina walks 0.85 mile to school. Kirk walks only 0.3 as far as Sabrina. How far does Kirk walk to school?

62. Isabel wrote 4 letters to her pen pals. For each letter she bought a stamp. Each stamp cost $0.60. How much did she spend on stamps?

63. Maura rode her bike 5 laps around the block. Each lap is 0.45 mile. How many miles did she ride?

64. Kim bought 2 pounds of baked turkey that cost $5.98 per pound. What was the total cost?

Multiply by Decimals

▶ Practice Multiplying Decimal Numbers Greater Than 1

Multiply.

1. $\begin{array}{r} 2.6 \\ \times\ 0.7 \\ \hline \end{array}$

3. $\begin{array}{r} 8.23 \\ \times\ \ 0.6 \\ \hline \end{array}$

3. $\begin{array}{r} 7.21 \\ \times\ \ 0.3 \\ \hline \end{array}$

4. $\begin{array}{r} 8.7 \\ \times\ 0.53 \\ \hline \end{array}$

5. $\begin{array}{r} 4.7 \\ \times\ 6.3 \\ \hline \end{array}$

6. $\begin{array}{r} 5.4 \\ \times\ 5.2 \\ \hline \end{array}$

7. $\begin{array}{r} 0.43 \\ \times\ 1.8 \\ \hline \end{array}$

8. $\begin{array}{r} 7.01 \\ \times\ 0.2 \\ \hline \end{array}$

9. $\begin{array}{r} 1.04 \\ \times\ 0.4 \\ \hline \end{array}$

10. $\begin{array}{r} 8.6 \\ \times\ 3.9 \\ \hline \end{array}$

11. $\begin{array}{r} 5.7 \\ \times\ 1.7 \\ \hline \end{array}$

12. $\begin{array}{r} 8.2 \\ \times\ 7.4 \\ \hline \end{array}$

13. $\begin{array}{r} 4.6 \\ \times\ 0.12 \\ \hline \end{array}$

14. $\begin{array}{r} 8.5 \\ \times\ 8.5 \\ \hline \end{array}$

15. $\begin{array}{r} 246.1 \\ \times\ \ .09 \\ \hline \end{array}$

16. $\begin{array}{r} 7.7 \\ \times\ 3.2 \\ \hline \end{array}$

17. $\begin{array}{r} 1.1 \\ \times\ 0.11 \\ \hline \end{array}$

18. $\begin{array}{r} 4.3 \\ \times\ 2.4 \\ \hline \end{array}$

19. $\begin{array}{r} 7.8 \\ \times\ 0.15 \\ \hline \end{array}$

20. $\begin{array}{r} 3.8 \\ \times\ 4.5 \\ \hline \end{array}$

▶ Solve Real World Problems

Solve.

21. Maggie is training to run in a 6-mile race. Her training program has her increase her weekly long run each week. This week she ran 4.5 miles. Next week she will run 1.3 times as far as she did this week. How far will she run next week?

22. Hank earned $140.95. Pellam earned 0.8 times as much as Hank did. How much did Pellam earn?

23. Tariq is building his dog a bed. He wants the width of his dog's bed to be .75 times as long as the length. If the length is 1.5 meters, how wide will the bed be?

24. The door to Sophia's room is 0.9 m wide and 2.06 m tall. In order to buy paint to paint it, she needs to know the area of one side of the door. What is the area of one side of her door?

Write an equation and then solve.

25. Adrienne and Evelyn have a pet cat. When they got it as a kitten, it weighed 0.6 kilograms. Now it weighs 7.3 times as much as it did when it was a kitten. How much does their cat weigh now?

26. The official weight of a U.S. penny is 2.5 grams. A quarter weighs a little more than 2.2 times as much as a penny. About how much does a quarter weigh?

Multiply with Decimals Greater Than 1

▶ Multiplication Properties

The **Commutative Property of Multiplication, Associative Property of Multiplication**, and **Distributive Property** can help you multiply.

Properties	
Commutative Property of Multiplication	$a \times b = b \times a$
Associative Property of Multiplication	$(a \times b) \times c = a \times (b \times c)$
Distributive Property	$a \times b + a \times c = a \times (b + c)$

Complete the equation and name the property used.

27. $4.5 \times 3.2 = \underline{\hspace{1.5cm}} \times 4.5$

28. $80 \times (72 \times 38) = (\underline{\hspace{1.5cm}} \times 72) \times 38$

29. $7 \times (3.8 + 4.2) = (7 \times \underline{\hspace{1.5cm}}) + (7 \times 4.2)$

30. $40 \times (50 \times 1.13) = (40 \times 50) \times \underline{\hspace{1.5cm}}$

31. $(3.2 \times 8.1) + (3.2 \times 1.9) = \underline{\hspace{1.5cm}} \times (8.1 + 1.9)$

32. $0.98 \times 2.6 = 2.6 \times \underline{\hspace{1.5cm}}$

33. Explain how you might use the properties to solve $25 \times (5.7 \times 4)$ mentally.

▶ Multiplication Properties (continued)

34. Explain how you might use the properties to solve
$(3.7 \times 8.2) + (1.8 \times 3.7)$ mentally.

35. Your calculator's battery is dead and you have to solve
this problem; $4 \times (7.3 \times 0.25)$. How can you make this
multiplication problem easier to solve?

▶ What's the Error?

Dear Math Students,

I need to solve this problem; $4 \times (2.5 \times 9.3)$.

I rewrote the problem using the Associative
Property of Multiplication to make it easier to
multiply;

$(4 \times 2.5) \times 9.3 = 10 \times 9.3 = 0.93$.
That answer doesn't seem right. Can you help
me find my error

Your friend,
Puzzled Penguin

36. Write a response to Puzzled Penguin.

Use Activity Workbook page 55.

▶ **Compare Whole Number and Decimal Multipliers**

Complete each sentence.

| **Whole Number Multipliers** | **Decimal Number Multipliers** |

1. When you multiply by 10, the number gets _____ times as great. The digits shift _____ place(s) to the _____.

2. When you multiply by 0.1, the number gets _____ as great. The digits shift _____ place(s) to the _____.

3. When you multiply by 100, the number gets _____ times as great. The digits shift _____ place(s) to the _____.

4. When you multiply by 0.01, the number gets _____ as great. The digits shift _____ place(s) to the _____.

5. How is multiplying by 10 or 100 like multiplying by 0.1 or 0.01? How is it different?

For each exercise, discuss the shift. Then find each product.

6. 3.6
    $\times$ 10

7. 3.6
    $\times$ 0.1

8. 3.6
    $\times$ 100

9. 3.6
    $\times$ 0.01

10. 0.48
     $\times$ 10

11. 5.6
     $\times$ 0.01

12. 2.49
     $\times$ 0.1

13. 1.7
     $\times$ 100

14. 0.6
     $\times$ 0.2

15. 0.9
     $\times$ 300

16. 0.9
     $\times$ 0.04

17. 0.6
     $\times$ 60

Use Activity Workbook page 56.

▶ Patterns in Multiplication by Powers of 10 Using Exponents

Recall that powers of 10, such as 10^1, 10^2, and 10^3 represent repeated multiplication with 10. The exponent tells you how many times to use 10 as a factor. The number of times 10 is used as a factor tells you how many places to shift the digits.

$10^1 = 10$ $10^2 = 10 \times 10 = 100$ $10^3 = 10 \times 10 \times 10 = 1{,}000$

$0.4 \times 10 = 0.4 \times 10^1 = \underline{\quad 4 \quad}$

$0.4 \times 100 = 0.4 \times 10 \times 10 = 0.4 \times 10^2 = \underline{\quad 40 \quad}$

$0.4 \times 1{,}000 = 0.4 \times 10 \times 10 \times 10 = 0.4 \times 10^3 = \underline{\quad 400 \quad}$

Study the pattern above. Then complete Exercises 18–25.

18. $0.8 \times 10 = 0.8 \times 10^1 = \blacksquare$

$0.8 \times 100 = 0.8 \times 10^2 = \blacksquare$

$0.8 \times 1{,}000 = 0.8 \times 10^3 = \blacksquare$

19. $0.27 \times 10 = 0.27 \times 10^1 = \blacksquare$

$0.27 \times 100 = 0.27 \times 10^2 = \blacksquare$

$0.27 \times 1{,}000 = 0.27 \times 10^3 = \blacksquare$

20. $4.8 \times 10^1 = \blacksquare$

$4.8 \times 10^2 = \blacksquare$

$4.8 \times 10^3 = \blacksquare$

21. $6.23 \times 10^1 = \blacksquare$

$6.23 \times 10^2 = \blacksquare$

$6.23 \times 10^3 = \blacksquare$

22. $0.49 \times 10^1 = \blacksquare$

$0.49 \times 10^2 = \blacksquare$

$0.49 \times 10^3 = \blacksquare$

23. $1.3 \times 10^1 = \underline{\blacksquare}$

$1.3 \times 10^2 = \underline{\blacksquare}$

$1.3 \times \underline{\blacksquare} = 1{,}300$

24. $0.84 \times 10^1 = \underline{\blacksquare}$

$0.84 \times \underline{\blacksquare} = 84$

$0.84 \times 10^3 = \underline{\blacksquare}$

25. $0.51 \times \underline{\blacksquare} = 5.1$

$0.51 \times 10^2 = \underline{\blacksquare}$

$0.51 \times 10^3 = \underline{\blacksquare}$

26. How is multiplying 0.07 by 10^2 like multiplying 7 by 10^2? How is it different?

Compare Shift Patterns

▶ What's the Error?

Dear Math Students,

My friend said that I didn't correctly complete the three equations shown below.

$6.08 \times 10^1 = 6.8$ $6.08 \times 10^2 = 68$ $6.08 \times 10^3 = 680$

What error did I make? Please help me find the correct products.

Your friend,
Puzzled Penguin

27. Write an answer to Puzzled Penguin.

Dear Math Students,

My teacher said that 0.8 kg $= 0.8 \times 10^3$ g. When I calculated how many grams that is, she said I had done it incorrectly. My answer was 0.8 kg $= 824$ g.

If I estimate the product, 0.8 times 100 is 80 so my answer seems reasonable. What error did I make? Please help me find the correct product.

Your friend,
Puzzled Penguin

28. Write an answer to Puzzled Penguin.

▶ Extend and Apply the Generalization

Zeros at the end of a decimal number do not change the value of the number. Remember this as you explore the generalization about the number of decimal places in a product.

These exercises all have an "extra" zero in the product because of the 5-pattern. **Complete each multiplication.**

29. $0.5 \times 2 =$ ▨   **30.** $0.08 \times 0.5 =$ ▨   **31.** $0.4 \times 0.5 =$ ▨

32. Does the generalization about the product having the same number of decimal places as the two factors still work?

These problems are all the same, but are expressed in different ways. **Multiply.**

33. $3 \times 3 =$ ▨   **34.** $3.0 \times 3 =$ ▨   **35.** $3.0 \times 3.0 =$ ▨

36. Does the generalization about the product having the same number of decimal places as the two factors still work? Do your answers all represent the same amount?

37.   40
       $\times\ 0.23$

38.   0.02
       $\times\ 0.3$

39.   400
       $\times\ 0.6$

40.   60
       $\times\ 1.7$

Show your work on your paper or in your journal.

41. Ada and her family are canoeing in the wilderness. They carry the canoe along trails between lakes. Their map gives each trail distance in rods. They know that a rod is equal to 5.5 yards. Find each trail distance in yards.

Black Bear Trail; 8 rods

Dark Cloud Trail; 24.1 rods

42. One of the world's largest diamonds is the Star of Africa, which is 530.2 carats. A carat is about 0.2 gram. What is the mass of the Star of Africa in grams?

▶ Review of Rounding

Round each number.

1. Round 42 to the nearest ten. Which ten is closer to 42?

50 ⌐
42
40 ⌐

2. Round 762 to the nearest hundred. Which hundred is closer to 762?

800 ⌐
762
700 ⌐

3. Round 0.86 to the nearest tenth. Which tenth is closer to 0.86?

0.9 ⌐
0.86
0.8 ⌐

4. Round 0.263 to the nearest hundredth. Which hundredth is closer to 0.263?

0.27 ⌐
0.263
0.26 ⌐

Round to the nearest ten.

5. 46   6. 71   7. 85   8. 928

Round to the nearest hundred.

9. 231   10. 459   11. 893   12. 350

Round to the nearest tenth.

13. 0.73   14. 0.91   15. 0.15   16. 0.483

Round to the nearest hundredth.

17. 0.532   18. 0.609   19. 0.789   20. 0.165

21. What is the greatest whole number that can be rounded to 30? What is the least?

22. What is the greatest decimal in hundredths that can be rounded to 14.5? What is the least?

► Explore Estimation in Multiplication

For each exercise, round the factors and multiply mentally to find the estimated answer. After finding all the estimated answers, go back and find each exact answer.

Estimated Answer   **Exact Answer**

23. $24 \times 39 \approx$ _____ $\times$ _____ $\approx$ _____ $24 \times 39 =$ _____

24. $151 \times 32 \approx$ _____ $\times$ _____ $\approx$ _____ $151 \times 32 =$ _____

25. $0.74 \times 0.2 \approx$ _____ $\times$ _____ $\approx$ _____ $0.74 \times 0.2 =$ _____

26. $12.3 \times 3.7 \approx$ _____ $\times$ _____ $\approx$ _____ $12.3 \times 3.7 =$ _____

27. Is there more than one way to round these numbers? Why are some exact answers closer to the estimated answer than others?

► Use Estimation to Check Answers

28. Tanya did these multiplications on her calculator.

$24.5 \times 4 = 98$	$0.56 \times 30 = 1.68$	$15.2 \times 2.03 = 30.856$
$0.09 \times 143 = 12.87$	$0.74 \times 12.2 = 90.28$	$9.03 \times 6.9 = 623.07$

How can she use estimation to see if each answer makes sense? Which answers are clearly wrong?

▶ Practice with Decimals

Suppose you know that 23 × 48 = 1,104. Use this to find each product.

1. 23 × 4.8 = ▨

2. 0.23 × 4.8 = ▨

3. 2.3 × 4.8 = ▨

4. 0.48 × 2.3 = ▨

5. 48 × 2.3 = ▨

6. 4.8 × 2.3 = ▨

7. 23 × 0.48 = ▨

8. 48 × 0.23 = ▨

Find each product.

9.　　46
　　× 0.9

10.　　75
　　× 0.8

11.　　97
　　× 0.04

12.　　64
　　× 0.05

13.　0.34
　　× 12

14.　　59
　　× 0.28

15.　　4.5
　　× 7.3

16.　0.92
　　× 0.8

17.　0.08
　　× 0.6

18.　0.53
　　× 0.4

19.　7.6
　　×0.3

20.　0.2
　　× 0.04

Show your
work on your paper
or in your journal.

▶ Solve Word Problems

Write an equation. Then solve. Check that your answers are reasonable.

21. Marcus sails his boat 4.5 miles every day. If he sails for 25 days, how far will he travel in all?

22. The distance around a circle (the circumference) is about 3.14 times the diameter. If a circular table has a diameter of 3 feet, what is the circumference?

23. Nina is reading about red kangaroos. She found out that a male red kangaroo usually weighs about 66 kilograms, and a female red kangaroo usually weighs about 26.5 kilograms. One kilogram is about 2.2 pounds. What is the weight of a male red kangaroo in pounds?

24. The 5th grade is getting a special lunch to celebrate the end of the first grading period. The cafeteria manager is planning to buy 0.3 pound of turkey for each student. If turkey is on sale for $0.79 per pound, what will it cost to give turkey to 100 students?

25. One U.S. gallon of water weighs 8.3 pounds. How much would 4.8 gallons weigh?

26. Guadalupe read an article that said the cost of driving a car 1 mile was about 57.5¢. She lives 0.6 mile from school. If the article is correct, what does it cost to drive Guadalupe to and from school every school day for a week?

▶ Math and Insects

Insects are sometimes called bugs, and are the most numerous living things on Earth.

There are nearly one million different kinds of known insects, and most scientists believe more than that number of insects have never been discovered and given names.

The table below shows typical lengths, in centimeters and inches, of interesting insects.

Emperor Dragonfly

Insect	Length	
	cm	in.
crazy ant	0.25	0.1
green stinkbug	1.5	0.6
walkingstick	25	10
megachile pluto bee	3.8	1.5
spotless ladybug	0.5	0.2
emperor dragonfly	7.8	3.1
praying mantis	10	4
giant water bug	11.6	4.6
firefly	1.9	0.75

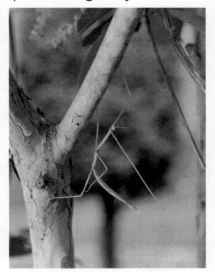

Walkingstick Insect

Solve. Use the table above.

1. Eight green stinkbugs, marching one behind the other, are about the same length in inches as which insect?

   Show your work on your paper or in your journal.

2. In centimeters, which insect is about forty times as long as a crazy ant?

3. The total length in inches of fifty spotless ladybugs is about the same length as which insect?

The table below shows typical wingspans, in centimeters and inches, of interesting flying insects.

Buckeye Butterfly

Insect	wingspan	
	cm	in.
confused cloudywing butterfly	3.2	1.26
Atlas moth	28	11.0
monarch butterfly	9	3.5
sleepy orange butterfly	4.5	1.8
damselfly	19.1	7.5
parasitic wasp	0.15	0.06
chickweed geometer moth	2.25	0.9
buckeye butterfly	5.7	2.24

Atlas Moth

Solve. Use the table above.

Show your work on your paper or in your journal.

4. In centimeters, which wingspan is twice as long as the wingspan of a chickweed geometer moth?

5. In inches, the total wingspan of six confused cloudywing butterflies is about the same as the wingspan of which insect?

6. How does the total wingspan in centimeters of 60 parasitic wasps compare to the wingspan of 2 sleepy orange butterflies?

7. An Atlas moth has a wingspan of 11 inches. Suppose the moth was placed on the cover of your math book. What is the difference between the length of the wingspan and your book?

8. Write and solve a problem of your own using data from the table.

Focus on Mathematical Practices

Use the Activity Workbook Unit Test on pages 57–58.

► **Vocabulary**

Choose the best term from the box.

1. The _____ is the number in a power that tells how many times the base is used as a factor. (**Lesson 4-1**)

2. _____ are the products of the smaller problems in the Place Value Sections or Rows methods. (**Lessons 4-3, 4-4**)

► **Concepts and Skills**

3. Explain how you know how many zeros will be in the product of 60×50? (**Lessons 4-1, 4-2**)

4. How is multiplying 0.3 by 10 like multiplying 0.3 by 0.1? How is it different? (**Lessons 4-1, 4-9**)

Multiply. (**Lessons 4-1, 4-7, 4-9**)

5. $400 \times 80 = $ ▨

6. $53 \times 100 = $ ▨

7. $20 \times 300 = $ ▨

8. $30 \times 0.1 = $ ▨

9. $0.04 \times 10 = $ ▨

10. $5.2 \times 100 = $ ▨

11. $56 \times 10^1 = $ ▨

$56 \times 10^2 = $ ▨

$56 \times 10^3 = $ ▨

12. $427 \times 10^1 = $ ▨

$427 \times 10^2 = $ ▨

$427 \times 10^3 = $ ▨

13. $0.6 \times 10^1 = $ ▨

$0.6 \times 10^2 = $ ▨

$0.6 \times 10^3 = $ ▨

14. $3.8 \times 10^1 = $ ▨

$3.8 \times 10^2 = $ ▨

$3.8 \times 10^3 = $ ▨

Multiply. Estimate to show your answers are reasonable.
(Lessons 4-4, 4-5)

15.	5,842	16.	413	17.	94	18.	63
	× 3		× 6		× 52		× 27

Multiply. Estimate to show your answers are reasonable.
(Lessons 4-6 to 4-10)

19.	8.7	20.	6.1	21.	0.7	22.	4.8
	× 3		× 7.5		× 0.9		× 0.7

▶ Problem Solving

Solve.

23. Each student collected 78 aluminum cans. There are 24 students in the class. How many cans did the class collect? (Lesson 4-11)

24. Max collected 80 aluminum cans. If the typical weight of an aluminum can is 14.2 grams, how much did his cans weigh altogether? (Lessons 4-11, 4-12)

25. **Extended Response** When you multiply 64.3 by 0.1, is the answer greater or less than 64.3? Explain.
(Lessons 4-9, 4-12)

Reference Tables

Table of Measures

Metric	Customary

Length/Area/Volume

Metric	Customary
1 millimeter (mm) = 0.001 meter (m)	1 foot (ft) = 12 inches (in.)
1 centimeter (cm) = 0.01 meter	1 yard (yd) = 36 inches
1 decimeter (dm) = 0.1 meter	1 yard = 3 feet
1 dekameter (dam) = 10 meters	1 mile (mi) = 5,280 feet
1 hectometer (hm) = 100 meters	1 mile = 1,760 yards
1 kilometer (km) = 1,000 meters	1 acre = 4,840 square yards
1 hectare (ha) = 1,000 square meters (m²)	1 acre = 43,560 square feet
1 square centimeter = 1 sq cm	1 acre = $\frac{1}{640}$ square mile
A metric unit for measuring area. It is the area of a square that is 1 centimeter on each side.	1 square inch = 1 sq in.
	A customary unit for measuring area. It is the area of a square that is 1 inch on each side.
1 cubic centimeter = 1 cu cm	1 cubic inch = 1 cu in.
A unit for measuring volume. It is the volume of a cube with each edge 1 centimeter long.	A unit for measuring volume. It is the volume of a cube with each edge 1 inch long.

Capacity

Metric	Customary
1 milliliter (mL) = 0.001 liter (L)	1 teaspoon (tsp) = $\frac{1}{6}$ fluid ounce (fl oz)
1 centiliter (cL) = 0.01 liter	1 tablespoon (tbsp) = $\frac{1}{2}$ fluid ounce
1 deciliter (dL) = 0.1 liter	1 cup (c) = 8 fluid ounces
1 dekaliter (daL) = 10 liters	1 pint (pt) = 2 cups
1 hectoliter (hL) = 100 liters	1 quart (qt) = 2 pints
1 kiloliter (kL) = 1,000 liters	1 gallon (gal) = 4 quarts

Mass / Weight

Mass	Weight
1 milligram (mg) = 0.001 gram (g)	1 pound (lb) = 16 ounces
1 centigram (cg) = 0.01 gram	1 ton (T) = 2,000 pounds
1 decigram (dg) = 0.1 gram	
1 dekagram (dag) = 10 grams	
1 hectogram (hg) = 100 grams	
1 kilogram (kg) = 1,000 grams	
1 metric ton = 1,000 kilograms	

Volume/Capacity/Mass for Water

1 cubic centimeter = 1 milliliter = 1 gram

1,000 cubic centimeters = 1 liter = 1 kilogram

Reference Tables (continued)

Table of Units of Time

Time

1 minute (min) = 60 seconds (sec)

1 hour (hr) = 60 minutes

1 day = 24 hours

1 week (wk) = 7 days

1 month is about 30 days

1 year (yr) = 12 months (mo)
or about 52 weeks

1 year = 365 days

1 leap year = 366 days

1 decade = 10 years

1 century = 100 years

1 millennium = 1,000 years

Table of Formulas

Perimeter

Polygon $P =$ sum of the lengths of the sides

Rectangle $P = 2(l + w)$ or $P = 2l + 2w$

Square $P = 4s$

Area

Rectangle $A = l \cdot w$

Square $A = s \cdot s$ or $A = s^2$

Volume of a Rectangular Prism

$$V = lwh \text{ or } V = Bh$$
(where B is the area of the base of the prism)

Properties of Operations

Associative Property of Addition

$(a + b) + c = a + (b + c)$ $(2 + 5) + 3 = 2 + (5 + 3)$

Commutative Property of Addition

$a + b = b + a$ $4 + 6 = 6 + 4$

Additive Identity Property of 0

$a + 0 = 0 + a = a$ $3 + 0 = 0 + 3 = 3$

Associative Property of Multiplication

$(a \cdot b) \cdot c = a \cdot (b \cdot c)$ $(3 \cdot 5) \cdot 7 = 3 \cdot (5 \cdot 7)$

Commutative Property of Multiplication

$a \cdot b = b \cdot a$ $6 \cdot 3 = 3 \cdot 6$

Multiplicative Identity Property of 1

$a \cdot 1 = 1 \cdot a = a$ $8 \cdot 1 = 1 \cdot 8 = 8$

Multiplicative Inverse

For every $a \neq 0$ there exists $\frac{1}{a}$ so that $a \cdot \frac{1}{a} = \frac{1}{a} \cdot a = 1$.

For $a = 5$, $5 \cdot \frac{1}{5} = \frac{1}{5} \cdot 5 = 1$.

Distributive Property of Multiplication over Addition

$a \cdot (b + c) = (a \cdot b) + (a \cdot c)$ $2 \cdot (4 + 3) = (2 \cdot 4) + (2 \cdot 3)$

Order of Operations

Step 1 Perform operations inside parentheses.

Step 2 Simplify powers.*

Step 3 Multiply and divide from left to right.

Step 4 Add and subtract from left to right.

*Grade 5 does not include simplifying expressions with exponents.

Problem Types

Addition and Subtraction Problem Types

	Result Unknown	Change Unknown	Start Unknown
Add to	A glass contained $\frac{2}{3}$ cup of orange juice. Then $\frac{1}{4}$ cup of pineapple juice was added. How much juice is in the glass now? *Situation and solution equation:*[1] $\frac{2}{3} + \frac{1}{4} = c$	A glass contained $\frac{2}{3}$ cup of orange juice. Then some pineapple juice was added. Now the glass contains $\frac{11}{12}$ cup of juice. How much pineapple juice was added? *Situation equation:* $\frac{2}{3} + c = \frac{11}{12}$ *Solution equation:* $c = \frac{11}{12} - \frac{2}{3}$	A glass contained some orange juice. Then $\frac{1}{4}$ cup of pineapple juice was added. Now the glass contains $\frac{11}{12}$ cup of juice. How much orange juice was in the glass to start? *Situation equation* $c + \frac{1}{4} = \frac{11}{12}$ *Solution equation:* $c = \frac{11}{12} - \frac{1}{4}$
Take from	Micah had a ribbon $\frac{5}{6}$ yard long. He cut off a piece $\frac{1}{3}$ yard long. What is the length of the ribbon that is left? *Situation and solution equation:* $\frac{5}{6} - \frac{1}{3} = r$	Micah had a ribbon $\frac{5}{6}$ yard long. He cut off a piece. Now the ribbon is $\frac{1}{2}$ yard long. What is the length of the ribbon he cut off? *Situation equation:* $\frac{5}{6} - r = \frac{1}{2}$ *Solution equation:* $r = \frac{5}{6} - \frac{1}{2}$	Micah had a ribbon. He cut off a piece $\frac{1}{3}$ yard long. Now the ribbon is $\frac{1}{2}$ yard long. What was the length of the ribbon he started with? *Situation equation:* $r - \frac{1}{3} = \frac{1}{2}$ *Solution equation:* $r = \frac{1}{2} + \frac{1}{3}$

[1]A situation equation represents the structure (action) in the problem situation. A solution equation shows the operation used to find the answer.

	Total Unknown	Addend Unknown	Other Addend Unknown
Put Together/ Take Apart	A baker combines $\frac{3}{4}$ cup of white flour and $\frac{1}{2}$ cup of wheat flour. How much flour is this altogether? *Math drawing:*[2] f $\frac{3}{4}$ $\frac{1}{2}$ *Situation and solution equation:* $\frac{3}{4} + \frac{1}{2} = f$	Of the $1\frac{1}{4}$ cups of flour a baker uses, $\frac{3}{4}$ cup is white flour. The rest is wheat flour. How much wheat flour does the baker use? *Math drawing:* $1\frac{1}{4}$ $\frac{3}{4}$ f *Situation equation:* $1\frac{1}{4} = \frac{3}{4} + f$ *Solution equation:* $f = 1\frac{1}{4} - \frac{3}{4}$	A baker uses $1\frac{1}{4}$ cups of flour. Some is white flour and $\frac{1}{2}$ cup is wheat flour. How much white flour does the baker use? *Math drawing:* $1\frac{1}{4}$ f $\frac{1}{2}$ *Situation equation* $1\frac{1}{4} = f + \frac{1}{2}$ *Solution equation:* $f = 1\frac{1}{4} - \frac{1}{2}$

[2]These math drawings are called math mountains in Grades 1—3 and break-apart drawings in Grades 4 and 5.

Problem Types continued

Addition and Subtraction Problem Types

	Difference Unknown	Greater Unknown	Smaller Unknown
Additive Comparison[1]	**Using "More"** At a zoo, the female rhino weighs $1\frac{3}{4}$ tons. The male rhino weighs $2\frac{1}{2}$ tons. How much more does the male rhino weigh than the female rhino? **Using "Less"** At a zoo, the female rhino weighs $1\frac{3}{4}$ tons. The male rhino weighs $2\frac{1}{2}$ tons. How much less does the female rhino weigh than the male rhino?	**Leading Language** At a zoo, the female rhino weighs $1\frac{3}{4}$ tons. The male rhino weighs $\frac{3}{4}$ tons more than the female rhino. How much does the male rhino weigh? **Misleading Language** At a zoo, the female rhino weighs $1\frac{3}{4}$ tons. The female rhino weighs $\frac{3}{4}$ tons less than the male rhino. How much does the male rhino weigh?	**Leading Language** At a zoo, the male rhino weighs $2\frac{1}{2}$ tons. The female rhino weighs $\frac{3}{4}$ tons less than the male rhino. How much does the female rhino weigh? **Misleading Language** At a zoo, the male rhino weighs $2\frac{1}{2}$ tons. The male rhino weighs $\frac{3}{4}$ tons more than the female rhino. How much does the female rhino weigh?

Difference Unknown

Math drawing:

$$2\frac{1}{2}$$

$$1\frac{3}{4} \qquad d$$

Situation equation:
$1\frac{3}{4} + d = 2\frac{1}{2}$ or
$d = 2\frac{1}{2} - 1\frac{3}{4}$

Solution equation:
$d = 2\frac{1}{2} - 1\frac{3}{4}$

Greater Unknown

Math drawing:

$$m$$

$$1\frac{3}{4} \qquad \frac{3}{4}$$

Situation and solution equation:
$1\frac{3}{4} + \frac{3}{4} = m$

Smaller Unknown

Math drawing:

$$2\frac{1}{2}$$

$$f \qquad \frac{3}{4}$$

Situation equation
$f + \frac{3}{4} = 2\frac{1}{2}$ or
$f = 2\frac{1}{2} - \frac{3}{4}$

Solution equation:
$f = 2\frac{1}{2} - \frac{3}{4}$

[1]A comparison sentence can always be said in two ways. One way uses *more*, and the other uses *fewer* or *less*. Misleading language suggests the wrong operation. For example, it says the *female rhino weighs $\frac{3}{4}$ tons less than the male*, but you have to add $\frac{3}{4}$ tons to the female's weight to get the male's weight

Multiplication and Division Problem Types[1]

	Unknown Product	Group Size Unknown	Number of Groups Unknown
Equal Groups	Maddie ran around a $\frac{1}{4}$-mile track 16 times. How far did she run? *Situation and solution equation:* $n = 16 \cdot \frac{1}{4}$	Maddie ran around a track 16 times. She ran 4 miles in all. What is the distance around the track? *Situation equation:* $16 \cdot n = 4$ *Solution equation:* $n = 4 \div 16$	Maddie ran around a $\frac{1}{4}$-mile track. She ran a total distance of 4 miles. How many times did she run around the track? *Situation equation* $n \cdot \frac{1}{4} = 4$ *Solution equation:* $n = 4 \div \frac{1}{4}$

	Unknown Product	Unknown Factor	Unknown Factor
Arrays[2]	An auditorium has 58 rows with 32 seats in each row. How many seats are in the auditorium? *Math drawing:* 32 58 | s *Situation and solution equation:* $s = 58 \cdot 32$	An auditorium has 58 rows with the same number of seats in each row. There are 1,856 seats in all. How many seats are in each row? *Math drawing:* s 58 | 1,856 *Situation equation:* $58 \cdot s = 1{,}856$ *Solution equation:* $s = 1{,}856 \div 58$	The 1,856 seats in an auditorium are arranged in rows of 32. How many rows of seats are there? *Math drawing:* 32 s | 1,856 *Situation equation* $s \cdot 32 = 1{,}856$ *Solution equation:* $s = 1{,}856 \div 32$

[1] In Grade 5, students solve three types of fraction division problems: 1) They divide two whole numbers in cases where the quotient is a fraction; 2) They divide a whole number by a unit fraction; 3) They divide a unit fraction by a whole number. Fraction division with non-unit fractions is introduced in Grade 6.

[2] We use rectangle models for both array and area problems in Grades 5 and 6 because the numbers in the problems are too large to represent with arrays.

Problem Types (continued)

Multiplication and Division Problem Types

	Unknown Product	Unknown Factor	Unknown Factor
Area	A poster has a length of 1.2 meters and a width of 0.7 meter. What is the area of the poster? Math drawing: 1.2 0.7 | A Situation and solution equation: $A = 1.2 \cdot 0.7$	A poster has an area of 0.84 square meters. The length of the poster is 1.2 meters. What is the width of the poster? Math drawing: 1.2 w | 0.84 Situation equation: $1.2 \cdot w = 0.84$ Solution equation: $w = 0.84 \div 1.2$	A poster has an area of 0.84 square meters. The width of the poster is 0.7 meter. What is the length of the poster? Math drawing: l 0.7 | 0.84 Situation equation $l \cdot 0.7 = 0.84$ Solution equation: $l = 0.84 \div 0.7$

	Unknown Product	Unknown Factor	Unknown Factor
Multiplicative Comparison	**Whole Number Multiplier** Sam has 5 times as many goldfish as Brady has. Brady has 3 goldfish. How many goldfish does Sam have? *Math drawing:* 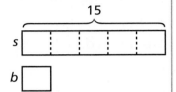 *Situation and solution equation:* $s = 5 \cdot 3$	**Whole Number Multiplier** Sam has 5 times as many goldfish as Brady has. Sam has 15 goldfish. How many goldfish does Brady have? *Math drawing:* 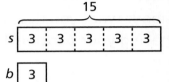 *Situation equation:* $5 \cdot b = 15$ *Solution equation:* $b = 15 \div 5$	**Whole Number Multiplier** Sam has 15 goldfish. Brady has 3 goldfish. The number of goldfish Sam has is how many times the number Brady has? *Math drawing:* 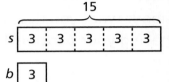 *Situation equation* $n \cdot 3 = 15$ *Solution equation:* $n = 15 \div 3$
	Fractional Multiplier Brady has $\frac{1}{5}$ times as many goldfish as Sam has. Sam has 15 goldfish. How many goldfish does Brady have? *Math drawing:* $\frac{1}{5}$ of 15 *Situation and solution equation:* $b = \frac{1}{5} \cdot 15$	**Fractional Multiplier** Brady has $\frac{1}{5}$ times as many goldfish as Sam has. Brady has 3 goldfish. How many goldfish does Sam have? *Math drawing:* 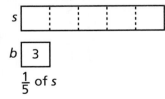 $\frac{1}{5}$ of s *Situation equation:* $\frac{1}{5} \cdot s = 3$ *Solution equation:* $s = 3 \div \frac{1}{5}$	**Fractional Multiplier** Sam has 15 goldfish. Brady has 3 goldfish. The number of goldfish Brady has is how many times the number Sam has? *Math drawing:* 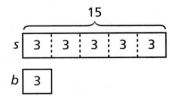 *Situation equation:* $n \cdot 15 = 3$ *Solution equation:* $n = 3 \div 15$

Vocabulary Activities

▶ Word Review   PAIRS

Work with a partner. Choose a word from a current unit or a review word from a previous unit. Use the word to complete one of the activities listed on the right. Then ask your partner if they have any edits to your work or questions about what you described. Repeat, having your partner choose a word.

Activities

▶ Give the meaning in words or gestures.

▶ Use the word in the sentence.

▶ Give another word that is related to the word in some way and explain the relationship.

▶ Crossword Puzzle   PAIRS OR INDIVIDUALS

Create a crossword puzzle similar to the example below. Use vocabulary words from the unit. You can add other related words, too. Challenge your partner to solve the puzzle.

¹d							
i		²s	u	m			
v		u					
i		b			³u		
⁴a	d	d	i	t	i	o	n
e		r			i		
n		a			t		
⁵a	d	d		c			
			t				
			i				
⁶g	r	o	u	p			
			n				

Across

2. The answer to an addition problem

4. _____ and subtraction are inverse operations.

5. To put amounts together

6. When you trade 10 ones for 1 ten, you _____.

Down

1. The number to be divided in a division problem

2. The operation that you can use to find out how much more one number is than another.

3. A fraction with a numerator of 1 is a _____ fraction.

▶ Word Wall   `PAIRS` OR `SMALL GROUPS`

With your teacher's permission, start a word wall in your classroom. As you work through each lesson, put the math vocabulary words on index cards and place them on the word wall. You can work with a partner or a small group to choose a word and give the definition.

▶ Word Web   `INDIVIDUALS`

Make a word web for a word or words you do not understand in a unit. Fill in the web with words or phrases that are related to the vocabulary word.

▶ Alphabet Challenge   `PAIRS` OR `INDIVIDUALS`

Take an alphabet challenge. Choose three letters from the alphabet. Think of three vocabulary words for each letter. Then write the definition or draw an example for each word.

Vocabulary Activities (continued)

▶ Concentration PAIRS

Write the vocabulary words and related words from a unit on index cards. Write the definitions on a different set of index cards. Mix up both sets of cards. Then place the cards facedown on a table in an array, for example, 3 by 3 or 3 by 4. Take turns turning over two cards. If one card is a word and one card is a definition that matches the word, take the pair. Continue until each word has been matched with its definition.

area

The number of square units that cover a figure.

▶ Math Journal INDIVIDUALS

As you learn new words, write them in your Math Journal. Write the definition of the word and include a sketch or an example. As you learn new information about the word, add notes to your definition.

rectangular prism: a solid figure with two rectangular bases that are congruent and parallel

volume: a measure of the amount of space occupied by a solid figure

▶ What's the Word? PAIRS

Work together to make a poster or bulletin board display of the words in a unit. Write definitions on a set of index cards. Mix up the cards. Work with a partner, choosing a definition from the index cards. Have your partner point to the word on the poster and name the matching math vocabulary word. Switch roles and try the activity again.

a point of reference used for comparing and estimating

estimate

round

mixed number

equivalent fraction

common denominator

benchmark

simplify a fraction

unsimplify a fraction

unit fraction

Glossary

acute triangle A triangle with three acute angles.

Examples:

additive comparison A comparison in which one quantity is an amount greater or less than another. An additive comparison can be represented by an addition equation.

Example: Josh has 5 more goldfish than Tia.

$$j = t + 5$$

area The number of square units that cover a two-dimensional figure without gaps or overlap.

Example:

Area = 3 cm × 5 cm = 15 sq. cm

Associative Property of Addition Changing the grouping of addends does not change the sum. In symbols, $(a + b) + c = a + (b + c)$ for any numbers a, b, and c.

Example:

$(4.7 + 2.6) + 1.4 = 4.7 + (2.6 + 1.4)$

Associative Property of Multiplication Changing the grouping of factors does not change the product. In symbols, $(a \cdot b) \cdot c = a \cdot (b \cdot c)$ for any numbers a, b, and c.

Example:

$(0.73 \cdot 0.2) \cdot 5 = 0.73 \cdot (0.2 \cdot 5)$

base In a power, the number that is used as a repeated factor.

Example: In the power 10^3, the base is 10.

benchmark A point of reference used for comparing and estimating. The numbers 0, $\frac{1}{2}$, and 1 are common fraction benchmarks.

centimeter (cm) A unit of length in the metric system that equals one hundredth of a meter. 1 cm = 0.01 m.

closed shape A shape that starts and ends at the same point.

Examples:

common denominator A common multiple of two or more denominators.

Example: 18 is a common denominator of $\frac{2}{3}$ and $\frac{5}{6}$.

$$\frac{2}{3} = \frac{12}{18} \text{ and } \frac{5}{6} = \frac{15}{18}$$

Commutative Property of Addition
Changing the order of addends does not change the sum. In symbols, $a + b = b + a$ for any numbers a and b.

Example: $\frac{3}{5} + \frac{4}{9} = \frac{4}{9} + \frac{3}{5}$

Commutative Property of Multiplication Changing the order of factors does not change the product. In symbols, $a \cdot b = b \cdot a$ for any numbers a and b.

Example: $\frac{3}{7} \cdot \frac{4}{5} = \frac{4}{5} \cdot \frac{3}{7}$

comparison A statement, model, or drawing that shows the relationship between two quantities.

comparison bars Bars that represent the greater amount and the lesser amount in a comparison situation.

Example: Sarah made 2 quarts of soup. Ryan made 6 quarts. These comparison bars show that Ryan made 3 times as many quarts as Sarah.

composite solid A solid figure made by combining two or more basic solid figures.

Example: The composite solid on the left below is composed of two rectangular prisms, as shown on the right.

concave polygon A polygon for which you can connect two points inside the polygon with a segment that passes outside the polygon. A concave polygon has a "dent."

Examples:

convex polygon A polygon that is not concave. All the inside angles of a convex polygon have a measure less than 180°.

Examples:

coordinate plane A system of coordinates formed by the perpendicular intersection of horizontal and vertical number lines.

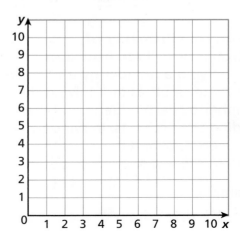

Glossary (continued)

cubic unit The volume of a unit cube. A cubic unit is a unit for measuring volume.

D

decimal A number that includes a decimal point separating the whole number part of the number from the fraction part of the number.

Examples:

7.3	seven and three tenths
42.081	forty-two and eighty-one thousandths

decimeter (dm) A unit of length in the metric system that equals one tenth of a meter. 1 dm = 0.1 m.

Digit-by-Digit Method A method for solving division problems.

Example:

```
      546
   7) 3,822
     -3,5
     ─────
       32
      -28
     ─────
       42
      -42
```

Distributive Property of Multiplication Over Addition
Multiplying a number by a sum gives the same result as multiplying the number by each addend and then adding the products. In symbols, for all numbers a, b, and c:
$a \times (b + c) = a \times b + a \times c$

Example:

$4 \times (2 + 0.75) = 4 \times 2 + 4 \times 0.75$

dividend The number that is divided in a division problem.

Example:

divisor The number you divide by in a division problem.

Example:

E

edge A line segment where two faces of a three-dimensional figure meet.

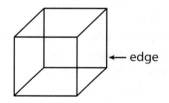

equilateral triangle A triangle with three sides of the same length.

Example:

equivalent decimals Decimals that represent the same value.

Example: 0.07 and 0.070 are equivalent decimals.

equivalent fractions Fractions that represent the same value.

Example: $\frac{1}{2}$ and $\frac{3}{6}$ are equivalent fractions.

estimate Find *about* how many or *about* how much, often by using rounding or benchmarks.

evaluate To substitute values for the variables in an expression and then simplify the resulting expression.

Example:

Evaluate $7 + 5 \cdot n$ for $n = 2$.

$7 + 5 \cdot n = 7 + 5 \cdot 2$ Substitute 2 for n.

$ = 7 + 10$ Multiply.

$ = 17$ Add

expanded form A way of writing a number that shows the value of each of its digits.

Example: The expanded form of 35.026 is $30 + 5 + 0.02 + 0.006$.

expanded form (powers of 10) A way of writing a number that shows the value of each of its digits using powers of 10.

Example: The expanded form of 35.026 using powers of 10 is

$(3 \times 10) + (5 \times 1) + (2 \times 0.01) +$
$(6 + 0.001)$

Expanded Notation Method A method for solving multidigit multiplication and division problems.

Examples:

```
    43
  × 67
 2,400
   280
   180
    21
 2,881
```

```
      6
     40 ⎤ 546
    500 ⎦
  7) 3,822
    −3,500
      322
     −280
       42
      −42
```

exponent In a power, the number that tells how many times the base is used as a factor.

Example: In the power 10^3, the exponent is 3.
$10^3 = 10 \times 10 \times 10$

exponential form The representation of a number that uses a base and an exponent.

Example: The exponential form of 100 is 10^2.

expression A combination of one or more numbers, variables, or numbers and variables, with one or more operations.

Examples: 4

t

$6 \cdot n$

$4 \div p + 5$

$5 \times 4 + 3 \times 7$

$6 \cdot (x + 2)$

F

face A flat surface of a three-dimensional figure.

face

factor One of two or more numbers multiplied to get a product.

Example:

$$\frac{3}{5} \cdot 10 = 6$$

factor   factor   product

Glossary (continued)

frequency table A table that shows how many times each outcome, item, or category occurs.

Example:

Outcome	Number of Students
1	6
2	3
3	5
4	4
5	2
6	5

G

greater than (>) A symbol used to show how two numbers compare. The greater number goes before the > symbol and the lesser number goes after.

Example: $\frac{2}{3} > \frac{1}{2}$ Two thirds is greater than one half.

H

hundredth A unit fraction representing one of one hundred equal parts of a whole, written as 0.01 or $\frac{1}{100}$.

I

isosceles triangle A triangle with at least two sides of the same length.

Examples:

L

less than (<) A symbol used to show how two numbers compare. The lesser number goes before the < symbol and the greater number goes after.

Example: $\frac{1}{4} < \frac{1}{3}$ One fourth is less than one third.

line plot A diagram that uses a number line to show the frequency of data.

Weight in Pounds

M

meter The basic unit of length in the metric system.

mile (mi) A customary unit of length equal to 5,280 feet or 1,760 yards.

millimeter (mm) A unit of length in the metric system that equals one thousandth of a meter. 1 mm = 0.001 m.

mixed number A number with a whole number part and a fraction part.

Example: The mixed number $3\frac{2}{5}$ means $3 + \frac{2}{5}$.

multiplier The number the numerator and denominator of a fraction are multiplied by to get an equivalent fraction.

Example: A multiplier of 5 changes $\frac{2}{3}$ to $\frac{10}{15}$.

multiplicative comparison

A comparison in which one quantity is a number of times the size of another. A multiplicative comparison can be represented by a multiplication equation or a division equation.

Example: Tomás picked 3 times as many apples as Catie.

$$t = 3 \cdot c$$

$$t \div 3 = c \text{ or } \frac{1}{3} \cdot t = c$$

N

New Groups Below Method A method used to solve multidigit multiplication problems.

Example:

$$
\begin{array}{r}
67 \\
\times\ 43 \\
\hline
{\scriptstyle 1\,2} \\
81 \\
{\scriptstyle 2\ 2} \\
480 \\
{\scriptstyle 1} \\
\hline
2{,}881
\end{array}
$$

numerical pattern A sequence of numbers that share a relationship.

Example: In this numerical pattern, each term is 3 more than the term before.

2, 5, 8, 11, 14, . . .

O

obtuse triangle A triangle with an obtuse angle.

Examples:

one-dimensional figure A figure with only one dimension, usually length.

Examples:

open shape A shape that does not start and end at the same point.

Examples:

Order of Operations A rule that states the order in which the operations in an expression should be done:

Step 1 Perform operations inside parentheses.

Step 2 Multiply and divide from left to right.

Step 3 Add and subtract from left to right.

ordered pair A pair of numbers that shows the position of a point on a coordinate plane.

Example: The ordered pair (3, 4) represents a point 3 units to the right of the y-axis and 4 units above the x-axis.

origin The point (0, 0) on the coordinate plane.

overestimate An estimate that is too big.

Glossary (continued)

P

parallelogram A quadrilateral with two pairs of parallel sides.

Examples:

partial products In a multidigit multiplication problem, the products obtained by multiplying each place value of one factor by each place value of the other.

Example: In the problem below, the partial products are in red.

$$25 \cdot 53 = 20 \cdot 50 + 20 \cdot 3 + 5 \cdot 50 + 5 \cdot 3$$

perimeter The distance around a figure.

Example:

Perimeter = $2 \cdot 3$ cm + $2 \cdot 5$ cm = 16 cm

Place Value Rows Method A method used to solve multidigit multiplication problems.

Example:

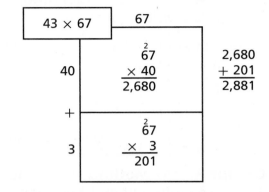

Place Value Sections Method A method used to solve multidigit multiplication and division problems.

Examples:

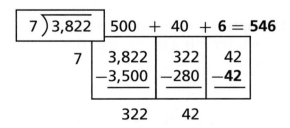

polygon A closed two-dimensional shape made from line segments that do not cross each other.

Examples:

power of 10 A power with a base of 10. A number in the form 10^n.

Examples: 10^1, 10^2, 10^3

product The result of a multiplication.

Example:

factor   factor   product

Q

quadrilateral A closed two-dimensional shape with four straight sides.

Examples:

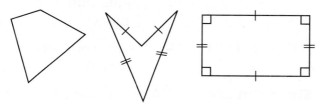

quotient The answer to a division problem.

Example:

dividend   divisor   quotient

R

rectangle A parallelogram with four right angles.

Examples:

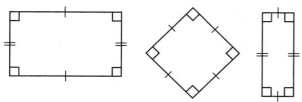

rectangular prism A solid figure with two rectangular bases that are congruent and parallel.

Example:

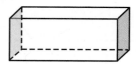

regular polygon A polygon in which all sides and all angles are congruent.

Examples:

remainder The number left over when a divisor does not divide evenly into a dividend.

Example:

$$\begin{array}{r} 13 \\ 7{\overline{\smash{)}94}} \\ -7 \\ \hline 24 \\ 21 \\ \hline 3 \end{array} \leftarrow \text{remainder}$$

rhombus A parallelogram with four congruent sides.

Examples:

Glossary (continued)

right triangle A triangle with a right angle.

Examples:

round To change a number to a nearby number.

Examples:

54.72 rounded to the nearest ten is 50.

54.72 rounded to the nearest one is 55.

54.72 rounded to the nearest tenth is 54.7.

$3\frac{7}{9}$ rounded to the nearest whole number is 4.

S

scalene triangle A triangle with no sides of the same length.

Examples:

shift To change position. When we multiply a decimal or whole number by 10, 100, or 1,000, the digits shift to the left. When we divide by 10, 100, or 1,000, the digits shift to the right. When we multiply by 0.1, 0.01, or 0.001, the digits shift to the right. When we divide by 0.1, 0.01, or 0.001, the digits shift to the left.

Examples:

$72.4 \times 100 = 7,240$	Digits shift left 2 places.
$5.04 \div 10 = 0.504$	Digits shift right 1 place.
$729 \times 0.01 = 7.29$	Digits shift right 2 places.
$0.26 \div 0.001 = 260$	Digits shift left 3 places.

Short Cut Method A method used to solve multidigit multiplication problems.

Example:

$$\begin{array}{r} \overset{1}{\underset{}{}}\overset{2}{\underset{}{}} \\ 43 \\ \times\ 67 \\ \hline 301 \\ 2,580 \\ \hline 2,881 \end{array}$$

simplify a fraction Make an equivalent fraction by dividing the numerator and denominator of a fraction by the same number. Simplifying makes fewer but larger parts.

Example: Simplify $\frac{12}{16}$ by dividing the numerator and denominator by 4.

$$\frac{12 \div 4}{16 \div 4} = \frac{3}{4}$$

simplify an expression Use the Order of Operations to find the value of the expression.

Example: Simplify $6 \cdot (2 + 5) \div 3$.

$$6 \cdot (2 + 5) \div 3 = 6 \cdot 7 \div 3$$
$$= 42 \div 3$$
$$= 14$$

situation equation An equation that shows the action or the relationship in a word problem.

Example:

Liam has some change in his pocket. He spends 25¢. Now he has 36¢ in his pocket. How much change did he have to start?

situation equation: $x - 25 = 36$

solution equation An equation that shows the operation to perform in order to solve a word problem.

Example:

Liam has some change in his pocket. He spends 25¢. Now he has 36¢ in his pocket. How much change did he have to start?

solution equation: $x = 36 + 25$

square A rectangle with four congruent sides. (Or, a rhombus with four right angles.)

Examples:

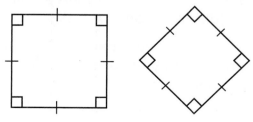

standard form The form of a number using digits, in which the place of each digit indicates its value.

Example: 407.65

T

tenth A unit fraction representing one of ten equal parts of a whole, written as 0.1 or $\frac{1}{10}$.

term Each number in a numerical pattern.

Example: In the pattern below, 3 is the first term, and 9 is the fourth term.

3, 5, 7, 9, 11, . . .

thousandth A unit fraction representing one of one thousand equal parts of a whole, written as 0.001 or $\frac{1}{1,000}$.

three-dimensional figure A figure with three dimensions, usually length, width, and height.

Examples:

ton (T) A customary unit of weight that equals 2,000 pounds.

trapezoid A quadrilateral with exactly one pair of parallel sides.

Examples:

Glossary (continued)

two-dimensional figure A figure with two dimensions, usually length and width.

Examples:

underestimate An estimate that is too small.

unit cube A cube with sides lengths of 1 unit.

1 unit
1 unit
1 unit

unit fraction A fraction with a numerator of 1. A unit fraction is one equal part of a whole.

Examples: $\frac{1}{3}$ and $\frac{1}{12}$

unsimplify Make an equivalent fraction by multiplying the numerator and denominator of a fraction by the same number. Unsimplifying makes more but smaller parts.

Example: Unsimplify $\frac{3}{4}$ by multiplying the numerator and denominator by 2.

$$\frac{3 \times 2}{4 \times 2} = \frac{6}{8}$$

variable A letter or other symbol used to stand for an unknown number in an algebraic expression.

volume A measure of the amount of space occupied by a solid figure. Volume is measured in cubic units.

word form The form of a number that uses words instead of digits.

Example: twelve and thirty-two hundredths

x-axis The horizontal axis of the coordinate plane.

x-coordinate The first number in an ordered pair, which represents a point's horizontal distance from the y-axis.

Example: The x-coordinate of the point represented by the ordered pair (3, 4) is 3.

y-axis The vertical axis of the coordinate plane.

y-coordinate The second number in an ordered pair, which represents a point's vertical distance from the x-axis.

Example: The y-coordinate of the point represented by the ordered pair (3, 4) is 4.